》Counselling the Intellectually Gifted Child《

Counselling the Intellectually Gifted Child

Avner Ziv

Guidance Centre   Faculty of Education   University of Toronto

First printing March, 1977
Second printing January, 1981

ISBN: 0-7713-0035-2

Design Peter Dorn

Printed and bound in Canada

The author and publishers wish to notify readers that the pronouns "he", "his", and "him" are frequently used in this book to refer to persons without specific reference to gender. This style was adopted for ease of writing, since the problems dealt with in the book are common to both sexes.

Guidance Centre
Faculty of Education
University of Toronto
Toronto, Ontario
M4W 2K8

Contents

Charts, Diagrams, and Tables

≫Counselling the Intellectually Gifted Child≪

Introduction

A few years ago I was working as a psychologist in a child-guidance clinic. A young mother, looking worried, entered my office one day to talk about a problem she was having with her small son, David. "David," she lamented, "simply refuses to go to school. Every morning we have an argument about it, and nearly every time it ends by his staying home." She looked up at me and added, "Frankly, I need help. David is only six now and in Grade One, and this is the way he's reacting to school. What is the future going to bring?"

I suggested that she have David come to see me. A few days later he stepped into my office, a blond, curly-haired, six-year-old boy with a freckled face and a mischievous smile that said "I know who *you* are."

David settled himself in a chair across from me, looked at me steadily, and said in a firm voice, "I know you want to convince me to go to school, and that you're going to give me many sound reasons why I should. I even know about a law that says six-year-olds have to go to school. I also know that my mother would be happy and reassured if I were to go. That *is* what you are going to tell me, isn't it?"

"Yes, David, you're quite right," I replied, puzzled and charmed all at once.

"Would you like to hear the reasons why I don't want to go to school?" Without waiting for my answer, he continued, "At home there are lots of wonderful books – whole shelves of them. I have books about birds and animals and people and the weather and countries, and all sorts of things. And I have two encyclopaedias and a dictionary. I think I like the science books the best. Right now I am reading Jules Verne's *Twenty Thousand Leagues Under the Sea*. Have you read it? It's fascinating, isn't it? I'm keeping a little scrapbook too. I put into my scrapbook all the things that interest me, and notes and conclusions from what I learn. I often use my daddy's microscope to see things that I can't see without it." Hardly pausing for breath, David went on, "Right now I'm spending a lot of time on a new project that I find exciting. Would you like to see what my project is?"

"Not quite yet," I said, wishing to hear and understand more of the boy's feelings about school.

But David already was standing beside me and handing me a scribbler. "That's it," he said proudly, pointing to pictures on the scribbler's cover, "the first modern electronic automatic toilet flusher. There's a sensor, connected to the reservoir, that opens the refill valve. There's no need to press buttons and no need to remember. It does it all for you."

I looked with amazement at the illustrations of circuit schemes on the scribbler cover. They all looked technical, very detailed, and very complicated. I opened the book and read on the first page, in large bold letters, "**THE CAT IS SAD. THE SAD CAT.**" There, in the contrast between the complexity of David's project and the simple sentences that teach first graders how to read, lay the stark reality to the boy's conflict. While pretending to adjust to the pace of his class, David had occupied himself at his own level and had relieved his boredom with spelling and the alphabet by the stratagem of inventing his mechanism.

I asked David whether he would like to play with some of the toys that were arranged on shelves in the room. His eyes lit up at the sight of a small airplane on a shelf nearby. David took the airplane, knelt on the floor, and "started" the engine with appropriate sound effects. Next he used building blocks to erect a toy airport that, in his imagination, became an actual, functioning entity under his sole control. In his play activity David was a six-year-old; obviously he loved playing. Suddenly he looked up, a happy smile on his face, and exclaimed, "You know, I do like going to school. Maybe you could arrange for me to go to school during recess, because recess is fun. If only recess weren't so short. My problem is that the time in class is long, and I get into trouble with the teacher. I already know what she tells us in class but she still wants me to do what the others are doing."

I was fascinated. Little David, so young, so small, but so full of strength. Yet that very strength, that particular giftedness of intellect, which helped him develop far beyond the children around him, could lead to his isolation.

This story started with a worried mother. It ends with a puzzled psychologist, faced with a problem to which he was unaccustomed. The mother wanted her child in school. I felt he should be in school. As I contemplated the reality of David's problem and the possible solutions, questions concerning children like David began to run through my mind:

What are the special characteristics of children like David? How do they adjust socially with children who do not have these special abilities?

How can I – or how should I – help a child like David find his place in school?

How should parents deal with a child like David?

Counselling the Intellectually Gifted Child

Are there many children whose superior intellect may create for them problems of personal and social adjustment?

What about other little Davids in schools elsewhere? How can they be identified and given help to prevent a lopsided, unhappy development in their environment?

What can a school offer to prevent the boredom of a child like David?

How can a classroom teacher deal with a child like David and with the thirty-odd other children in the class who lack his intellectual needs?

What about children with superior intellects who are subject to special disadvantages?

The text which follows records ideas and possible answers to these questions. The first part will provide a conceptual frame of reference for understanding intellectual giftedness. This is done in four chapters. Chapter 1 surveys the conflicting views which our society tends to hold of the numerically small, but significant, segment who are intellectually gifted. It is clear that the gifted have the potential to provide important resources, as well in the intellectual fields as in leadership fields as in leadership for society. It is equally clear that society regards the gifted with suspicion, and with attitudes which are frequently prejudiced, negative, and lacking foundation in fact. Chapter 2 defines the term "intellectual giftedness," as it is used in this book, and discusses some of the problems inherent in discovering the degree of mental superiority which the term implies. Chapter 3 summarizes scientific research on the gifted by such twentieth-century psychologists as Lewis M. Terman and Leta S. Hollingsworth. The section ends with a chapter presenting some of the special traits and needs which tend to be characteristic of gifted children.

The second part puts forward some concrete ways to help the gifted. Chapter 5, presents problems of underachievement, social relations, and emotional adjustment which confront some children because of their superior mental ability. These children require, not a special kind of counselling, but the good counselling which all children need. Chapter 6 deals with methods, tools, and suggested techniques for the collaboration of counsellors, teachers, parents, and classmates in obtaining inestimable information to assist in the identification of gifted children. The gifted child needs an extra something to satisfy his intellectual appetite; Chapter 7 describes various special programs for such children based on grouping, acceleration, and enrichment, and a novel community approach. The advantages and disadvantages of each type of program are outlined to help counsellors decide which approach would be most suitable for a particular child. This part concludes with a description of two groups of gifted children who are under a disadvantage and unlikely to fulfil their potential either because they are from different cultural backgrounds or because they are girls.

This book is written for counsellors, psychologists, teachers (and students learning about children), parents, and, in fact, for all those who are interested in children. Some readers may be impatient with the numbers in the text referring to the Chapter Notes and Bibliography; they are probably not interested in the many titles of books and articles. Others, I hope, will become more interested in gifted children and will want to learn more about them. The Bibliography, then, could be very helpful.

Gifted children form a valuable part of our society. They need scope and material on which their intellect and imagination can feed. They need active encouragement and appropriately balanced outlets for their superior intelligence. Yet they are still children with all the basic needs of children. It is my hope that this book will provide some understanding of intellectual giftedness in children and that it will furnish guidance for the satisfaction of the special needs and requirements of the gifted.

A.Z.

I
»The Intellectually Gifted«

1   Society's Views of Intellectual Giftedness

Giftedness is found in all human activity. There are gifted cooks and football players as surely as there are gifted novelists and scientists. Simply, giftedness is human excellence. For our purposes, however, we have chosen to focus on one aspect only of human excellence; intellectual giftedness. Our assumption – and it is only an assumption – is that from the intellectually gifted come those profound changes which are most likely to affect all of society. Without disparaging the achievements of a gifted cook, we nevertheless believe that the contributions of an Einstein or, at a less exalted level, of an economist, who can shape patterns of consumption and distribution, are probably of a more lasting nature. The reason for our assumption is to be found in the conditions of the twentieth century.

Demand for intellectual talent is an inevitable result of present society's level of development. As Alfred North Whitehead wrote: "In condition of modern life a rule is absolute, the race which does not value trained intelligence is doomed."[1] The continually accelerating rate of unpredictable changes in the twentieth century is described dramatically by Alvin Toffler in *Future Shock*.[2] It is indisputable that we need persons of high ability who are educationally prepared to deal with the rampant proliferation of problems concomitant with these changes. If special efforts are not made to identify, train, and utilize those who are intellectually superior, the results could be devastating to the whole world.

Of course, our generation is not the first to be concerned about the utilization of intellectual resources; most historians argue that every society has thought of itself as facing crucial problems which require maximum employment of its especially gifted citizens. Even in ancient Greece, Plato proposed in *The Republic* that special attempts should be made to identify gifted children among all social classes so that they could be educated as leaders of the state. Plato wrote:

> The first duty which the gods have placed upon the rulers is to scrutinize every child from birth and to see what kind of metal enters the composition of their souls; they are then to select all the children of gold, whether they come from parents of gold, or (as may occasionally happen) from parents of silver, iron or even bronze.

But the attempts throughout history to identify these "children of gold" and to foster their intellectual giftedness were largely inadequate and resulted in the creation of primitive and unscientific concepts of the meaning of gifted. Not until 1921, when Lewis Terman began his research, was the area of scientific study of giftedness begun.*

We can identify three broad approaches to the concept of giftedness. The first may be designated as the psychopathological approach. The second attempts to define the gifted in terms of their social impact, as seen in an historical perspective. And finally, the third approach sees the gifted in a statistical framework.

The psychopathological approach confined intellectual superiority to a form of mental disorder, therefore likening genius to imbecility. Lombroso, in 1891, described case studies that suggested that genius was a kind of degenerative psychosis of the epileptoid group. In the same year, Nisbet published case histories of famous men and arrived at the same conclusions as Lombroso. This view has been slow in disappearing, as Burt noted in 1962.[3] It was defended in 1951 by Kretchmer in his book *The Psychology of Men of Genius*,[4] and as recently as 1960 by Russell Brain. In *Some Reflections on Genius*, Brain describes genius as a nervous abnormality.[5] Adler's perception of genius as a compensation for a feeling of inferiority and Freud's view that the creative process is a result of fixation of early infantile desires are also attitudes that question the mental health of gifted persons.

According to the social-historical approach, the gifted are defined by the enduring impact of their contributions to society, as viewed from a long-range perspective. It is true that many talented people *do* have an impact on contemporary society, but it is questionable as to how "gifted" these people really are. At the moment, Jacqueline Susann's works are read by more people than are those of William Shakespeare. However, in the social-historical approach, we are not in a position to judge whether she will be classed eventually in the same gifted category as Shakespeare. In addition, the social-historical approach assumes that it is not possible to decide if a *child* is gifted, for an individual's impact on society can be judged only after a long period of time, and rarely during his or her lifetime.

The statistical approach defines giftedness in terms of mental ability in relation to the rest of the population. Mental ability, as measured by psychometric tests, is distributed according to the normal curve. At one end of the curve, representing approximately 3 per cent of the population, are those considered gifted; at the other end are the severely mentally retarded, who also constitute approximately 3 per cent of the population.

*My own scholarly background predisposes me to take a long historical tour of the major philosophical doctrines concerning treatment of the intellectually gifted. I will refrain and suggest instead that the interest reader consult Gertrude H. Hildreth, *Introduction to the Gifted* (New York: McGraw-Hill, 1966), pp. 41-52.

Counselling the Intellectually Gifted Child

Despite the fact that the gifted and the mentally retarded occur in similar proportions in the general population, it seems that society, at least in recent times, has been much more concerned with the latter group. Why is this so?

From a behavioural perspective, it is not difficult to recognize mentally retarded children, for these individuals visibly lack the requirements necessary to perform adequately in their natural environments. Intelligence tests are not essential to identify these children, but the qualities which differentiate gifted children are less obvious. Gifted children create far fewer problems; whatever concern they cause is surely of a different kind, because they are the individuals who require the least attention, the least help in their studies. Another possible reason is the sense of social responsibility which figures predominantly in our culture. Since we know that the retarded cannot be self-reliant, there is an unwritten social commitment to assume a certain degree of responsibility for them. The concern of society is not entirely altruistic, for it benefits from the maximum utilization of its available manpower; after appropriate training, many mentally retarded people can work at semi-skilled occupations. Without educational intervention, some of these people would become burdens upon society. The gifted, apparently, pose no such danger, and their special needs are overlooked.

It is clear, then, that it is in the economic self-interest of society to train the retarded and thereby assist them to become self-sufficient. But does commitment to aiding the retarded signify that the gifted should be overlooked? Of course, nothing of the sort is necessarily implied. But there are some beliefs imbedded rather deeply in western society which have resulted in the ignoring of the gifted.

First there is what John Gardner defines as a mistaken conception of egalitarianism, by which society chooses to ignore the most capable and intelligent of its members or to reduce them to the level of the average.[6] In short, egalitarianism in practice means that we overlook the gifted, because, in theory, they are not supposed to exist.

There is a second reason: recognition of the existence of the gifted is threatening. It is humane to assist the retarded; by definition they are persons who need help. But, to admit that there are people who are gifted, is to admit that there are people who are smarter and more capable than oneself. And this is psychologically troublesome.

These reasons explain why, despite the improvement in techniques for identifying the formerly less visible, superior pupil, our investments have remained largely with the mentally retarded. This state of affairs exists not only in the economic area, where the financial investment in special programs for the retarded is astonishingly larger than in those for the gifted, but also in the field of research, where energy invested in the retarded is markedly greater. For instance, in the 1975 *Psychological Abstracts* there are 811 entries concerning the mentally-retarded and only 54 entries concerning the gifted. We agree that help and advancement of the mentally retarded is a very important social responsibility. But we must seriously question whether our society can allow itself to neglect the identification, support, and guidance of the gifted, particularly when we consider the significant contributions of these individuals.

In his follow-up study of 800 gifted children 25 years afterwards, Lewis Terman reported that by 1950, when the average age of the group was 40 years, the group members had published 67 books, nearly 1,700 articles on a wide variety of subjects, and over 200 short stories and plays, as well as an impressive quantity of material for newspapers, radio, and television. They had also taken out over 150 patents.

Educationally, over half of the 800 men in the group had achieved significant status. This included 78 PH.D. or equivalent degrees and 48 medical and 85 law degrees. 74 had taught or were then teaching in a four-year college or university; 51 had done basic research in the physical sciences or engineering; and 104, who were engineers, had done only applied research. The proportionate record of achievement was 20 to 30 times higher than that which would be attained by a group of similar size selected at random.

Terman concluded that these facts were an adequate answer to those who disparage the significance of differences in I.Q.'s, and their predictive value.[7]

These impressive results direct attention to the contributions of the gifted. On superficial inspection, one might conclude that these gifted children developed naturally into gifted adults. However, as we shall see later, closer examination of Terman's study reveals important differences between the gifted children who fulfilled their potential as adults and those who did not.

We know about the people who have contributed to society's greatest achievements. We know, for example, about gifted individuals such as Edison, Einstein, and Churchill who were able to surmount discouragement caused by their environment in their younger years. Thomas Edison was at the bottom of his class; his father thought him dull. Albert Einstein had to repeat a class, because his mathematics teacher considered him not intelligent enough to understand mathematics. (This error in judgement ensured the teacher's own place in history.) It has been said that his teacher regarded Sir Winston Churchill as a below-average pupil, and a special failure in English.

Counselling the Intellectually Gifted Child

Luckily for them, and for us, these individuals were strong enough to persevere and realize tremendous achievements.

But we do not know about those who possessed the necessary intellectual potential, but could not realize it because of environmental pressures. What about those gifted individuals who believed their teachers or who, for various reasons were not able to continue their studies or their activities in the chosen field. One can assume that many such cases existed in the past, and that they exist today as well.

Some data on the loss of talent in the United States were presented in a paper by D. L. Thistlewhite, in 1958.[8] According to his research and that of others published and surveyed by him, it appears that 39 per cent of the high school graduates who score among the top 2.8 per cent on intelligence tests, do not attend college, and 30 per cent of public high school seniors who score among the highest 10 per cent on aptitude tests, do not attend college. Thistlewhite also estimated that about 28 per cent of the top ten of American high school graduates did not attend university as full-time students.

This waste of high intellectual potential may have tremendous implications for society. As William James noted in 1906:

> The world . . . is only beginning to see that the wealth of a nation consists of the superior men that it harbors.[9]

The relevance of his observation has not decreased; nor has our attention to the problem itself increased.

Interest in the gifted fluctuates with international crises. The most notable of these recent shifts occurred after the Soviet Union launched Sputnik, the first space satellite, in 1956. In the United States, the launch was followed immediately by dire warnings of impending catastrophe to the nation, unless action were taken to revitalize its educational system. It would be necessary to catch up technologically with the Russians in order to restore the balance of power. Although the impact of this event was reflected in the curricula at all levels of education and for all children and youth of at least normal intelligence, the main targets of the "movement" were the most intelligent, especially those with scientific talents. In his book, *Educating the Gifted*, Joseph L. French notes that there were thirty times as many articles on the gifted published in the three years after Sputnik, as in the previous ten years.[10] Yet, it appears that when their self-confidence had been restored by subsequent technological advances, Americans reverted to their former stance toward the gifted. A count of the articles cited in *Psychological Abstracts* since 1968 shows that research on the gifted has decreased since the Sputnik era. The dearth of research and the lack of training programs for teachers of the gifted seem to indicate that we are once again merely paying lip-service to the gifted.

From all that has been said, the need for paying organized and concentrated attention to the gifted should be apparent. We need to identify children with potential, and to foster their abilities, and we need to do so at an early stage. Furthermore, the importance of early discovery of superior abilities has been highlighted by the facts disclosed by Harvey Lehman, in his investigation of the relation between age and creative achievement.[11] It appears that in almost all fields of science, the best work is done between the ages of twenty-five and thirty-five (and rarely past forty). From these statistics, it would seem crucial to prepare the gifted youth for attainment of his highest potential before too many of these precious creative years have vanished. We need to prevent parents, schools, and peers, who are unaware of the gifted child's special characteristics, from causing irreparable damage by attempting to force the child into the stereotyped role of the average youngster.

We need to decide what "giftedness" means and the methods to be used for its measurements. These questions will form the topics of the next chapter.

In order to identify something, it is helpful to know what it is you are seeking. As strange as it may seem, it is easier to identify mental abilities, than it is to define them. Although the attempts to define the term "intelligence" have been numerous and varied, none have, as yet, yielded a definition that is generally accepted.

One courageous attempt to arrive at the "true" definition of intelligence was made in 1921 by the editor of the *Journal of Educational Psychology*. He invited seventeen leading American psychologists working in research on intelligence to answer two questions:

1 What is intelligence and what is the best measurement for it in groups?
2 What are the most critical next steps?

Thirteen of these psychologists prepared articles, and excerpts from a few of them illustrate the breadth of the concept of intelligence and the divergence in definition. Terman for instance, believed that "an individual is intelligent in proportion as he is able to carry on abstract thinking."[1] And he distinguished various levels of intellectual functioning. Thorndike stressed the interrelationship of all human functions – mental abilities, physical abilities, interest, and the like – and defined intelligence as "the power of good responses from the point of view of truth or fact."[2] Thorndike held that it would be impossible to construct a battery of tests to measure all human mental ability, and he expressed a need for intelligence tests of all types. Terman went a step further and urged the use of "outside criteria," or performance in life situations, to validate measures of intelligence.

Colvin criticized the definition of general intelligence as "general mental adaptability to new problems and conditions of life" as being too broad and too narrow. He believed that a person is intelligent to the extent that "he has learned or can learn to adjust himself to his environment. This includes the capacity for getting along well in all sorts of situations."[3] Pintner based himself on these criteria and defined intelligence as the "ability of the individual to adapt himself adequately to relatively new situations in life."[4]

Why does the definition of intelligence provoke all this controversy among scholars? Is intelligence something so obscure or so elusive? Is it a word that has so many meanings, that, in fact, it has none? How, then do we establish whether one definition of intelligence is better than another? In his paper, "On Defining Intelligence," Miles started by trying to define the word "definition." He found no fewer than twelve definitions for it, each with special reference to the problem of defining intelligence.[5] It follows that a formulation of intelligence is justified when relevant to the type of definition expressed.

The fact that the experts did not agree on a definition of intelligence did not prevent them from continuing to measure this quality energetically. As a matter of fact, research and theories about human intelligence have been the most disputed and the most important contributions made within the science of psychology. Different views or approaches on intelligence have generated different types of theories.

For our purposes, however, we need not make a choice among the many competing theories concerning intelligence. If there is still no universal consensus after seventy-five years of intense effort by a great many able researchers, we shall have to bypass a definitive definition of intelligence and intellectual giftedness, and fall back on a more obvious and somewhat easier solution. We shall attempt to arrive at intellectual ability by looking at what society has already labelled as intellectual giftedness. We shall see that society has, in effect, already decided that the intellectually gifted are those who have created something; the intellectually gifted person is identified by examining a particular product.

The gifted scientist creates a theory of relativity; the gifted chemist invents a significant process; the gifted mathematician devises an important mathematical concept; the gifted economist produces an idea which affects the way in which the whole nation lives. We can, then, judge who is gifted by examining the product which he creates. And this is the problem: we know who the gifted adults are, but not who the gifted children are. For adults, giftedness is a product; for children, it is a promise, since children do not usually invent socially significant products. Our judgements about giftedness in children have always been hazy.

There may well be intellectually gifted shepherds in a pastoral culture, but they will be difficult to locate. In our society, schools diminish the difficulty of distinguishing intellectual giftedness, for schools are pre-eminently places for intellectual activities. A school is a place where people are asked to add numbers, to memorize poems or formulas, to write essays, or to analyze concepts. Children are routinely required to manipulate symbols, to quantify amounts, and to engage in other activities most of us label "intellectual." Those who do these activities unusually well are called "gifted." But, herein lies another problem: exactly how do teachers decide who performs these activities unusually well?

Teachers do evaluate, and they evaluate constantly. Evaluation is expressed in a variety of ways: letters, numbers, percentage points, and even little gold stars. If such evaluations did indeed reflect the degree of utilization of high mental abilities, we would be able to differentiate easily between those children with high abilities and those whose abilities are low. We know, however, that a teacher's evaluation does not always reflect a one-to-one correspondence. A massive amount of research done during this century, suggests very strongly that teachers' evaluations are likely to be influenced by factors which are probably irrelevant. Indeed, teachers often are unlikely to make important discriminations as to *how* students approach a problem. Let us discuss two hypothetical situations and compare and contrast the ways in which the problem is attacked and solved.

Two children, Jonathan and Danny, are both faced with the same assignment in history. Jonathan takes the faster way out: he wants to find all the answers word for word in his book. An unanswered question is to him not a challenge or an opportunity; it is a nuisance. His whole approach to this assignment is grade-oriented. If he cannot find an answer, he wants to be told the answer by someone who does know. Whether or not he understands the answer, let alone assimilates it, is of no concern to him.

Danny, on the other hand, embraces his assignment; it becomes a project, part of him. He takes time to understand it fully. He can admit to himself that some answers are hard to find, but he himself wants to struggle with them. When his assignment is completed, it often incorporates creative, but not always desired, material on related interesting questions which Danny explored on the way.

The same two children are then assigned a simple problem in algebra. Jonathan might conjure up a combination of bits of formulas which he recalls from the solution of somewhat similar problems; by a trial-and-error changing of what he remembers, he "guesses" the right answer. Danny, on the other hand, attacks the problem by creating it whole in his mind, and by thinking about the situation until, in a rapid and systematic way, he discovers an algebraic formula which leads him to the solution. In both situations, it is then the teacher's responsibility to give a quantitative value to the children's intellectual efforts. Both children may receive the same grade for each of the assignments, but do their grades represent how well they learned? Furthermore, so many elements from the sphere of personality – impressions, attractions, and preferences – come into play when a teacher evaluates the work of a child. School grades are supposed to be an unbiased measure of the intellectual achievement of a child. In reality, they are influenced by many non-intellectual elements.

Let us look at two other children, Eve, and Adam. Eve is neat, polite, attentive, and punctual. Adam is wild, mischievous, noisy and invariably tardy. He never seems to know what is going on in the class. Eva brings her homework to school, neatly enclosed in a folder with her name clearly marked at the top. Adam, after a lot of fumbling through his school bag, starts a full-fledged search through his desk. Only after the teacher threatens to send a note home, does Adam remember that he stuffed his homework in his back pocket. Are we surprised then, to learn that the two children received different grades, even though, in fact, they did the assignment together and handed in very similar results.

Behaviour is not the only element which differentiates these two children. In a classic 1959 study, Meyer and Thompson showed that an unconscious sex bias exists among teachers. The authors found that female teachers gave a significantly higher number of "disapprovals" to boys than they did to girls. They interpreted their findings as "supporting the notion that teachers are responding to the greater expression of aggression by boys."[6] It was also found that boys perceive that they receive more blame than do girls. Is it then possible that exhibited disobedience, such as Adam's, is a reaction to this perceived bias?

An additional drawback of grades is the fact that they very often are a function of different grading philosophies among teachers. Everyone who thinks back nostalgically or loathingly to his school days, must certainly remember how some teachers assigned grades. Some were stingy, others were generous, and some were simply bizarre. The author still shudders when he remembers the teacher who explained his grading philosophy in the following way. When he returned the assignments he said, "One hundred is for a perfect job. Since nobody is perfect, nobody gets 100. Since I know a great deal more than all of you, I am graded in the 90's. Therefore the best grade you can get is 89." Other teachers maintain that high grades encourage superior achievement. They show their good intentions by giving hundreds of "100" marks.

In sum, there is too much variability in the grading process. Philosophies of grading vary from school to school and from teacher to teacher. Children are evaluated under dissimilar conditions. Different values are assigned to the same aspect of performance. Culture, sexual bias, personal standards of neatness, and other irrelevant factors intrude.

This state of affairs was recognized in Paris in the late nineteenth century, where the French Ministry of Education turned to a psychologist, Alfred Binet, for the solution to a very practical problem: "Why are so many young French children failing school?" The Minister wanted Binet to devise a precise and accurate measure that would indicate those children unable to profit from normal schooling. Since the danger of relying on school grades was known even in 1904, Binet designed the test with standardized instructions. The test was to be given under the same conditions for all children and was objective in administration and scoring. It was based on the conception that intelligence is an ability which develops with age. Binet and his co-author Simon collected and devised a large number of questions and problems and administered them to children of different age levels. They found that most of the children of a certain age were capable of solving problems to a certain level of difficulty but could not solve more difficult ones. The level of problems solved by 75 per cent of the children in the normal population was considered to indicate the *mental age*. A child able to solve the problems solved by 75 per cent of the children of age 10 – but no more – has a mental age of 10, no matter what his chronological age is. The intelligence quotient or, as it is better known, the I.Q., is the relation between mental age and chronological age. It is calculated according to the following formula:

$$\frac{MA}{CA} \times 100 = IQ$$

where M.A. means mental age, and C.A. means chronological age.

Let us take three children whose chronological age is eight. The first child solves the problems on the Binet test whch gives him a mental age of eight. His I.Q. is 8/8 × 100 = 100. The second child solves problems that give him a mental age of six. His I.Q. is 6/8 × 100 = 75. The I.Q. of the third one, with a mental age of ten, is 10/8 × 100 = 125.

Intelligence quotient is distributed according to the normal curve, and the percentage of the population falling into the different levels is represented in Figure 1.

Fig. 1   DISTRIBUTION OF INTELLIGENCE QUOTIENT BY PERCENTAGE
OF POPULATION

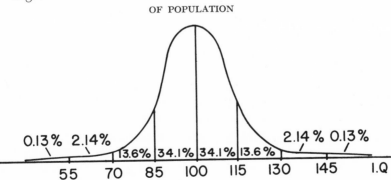

As can be seen, the majority of the population, 68.2 per cent, has an I.Q. between 85 and 115. The levels of intelligence may be classified in the following way:

I.Q. under 75	Mentally retarded
I.Q. from 76 to 90	Slow learners
I.Q. from 91 to 110	Normal intelligence
I.Q. from 111 to 130	Above normal or superior intelligence
I.Q. above 130	Gifted

Some authors[7] distinguish between several levels of high ability in the following way:

Academically superior	Above 115 I.Q. (16 per cent of population)
Superior	Above 125 I.Q. (5 per cent of population)
Gifted (Terman)	Above 140 I.Q. (0.6 per cent of population)
Highly gifted	Above 160 I.Q. (0.007 per cent of population)

For our purposes, we shall consider as gifted those having an I.Q. above 130. As we have seen, persons in this category make up almost 3 per cent of the population.

How are I.Q. levels reflected in actual behaviour? An eight-year-old child with an I.Q. of 70 may be normal in size and appearance. He has, however, the mental capacity of a five-and-a-half year old and is hardly ready to learn how to read. If he is put in the third grade he may be teased and humiliated; he cannot hold his own with children his own age. On the other hand, an eight-year-old child with an I.Q. of 130 has the mental capacity of a ten-and-a-half year old. He too, may encounter problems in adjusting to his age group. He learns quickly; he may be bored with the activities of his class, and he may work off his excess energy in mischief. He may want to compete with older children and be rejected by them, or he may boss children his own age. Physically, and emotionally he is still an eight-year old.

But children having the same I.Q. are equally likely to be different in their behavioural patterns and intellectual capacities. The I.Q. does not tell the whole story. In order to understand the real meaning of an I.Q., one must understand the kinds of mental abilities which are measured with the particular intelligence test. Literally hundreds of intelligence tests exist. Some of the tests have been constructed according to a particular theory. The theory of Spearman, which stresses

Counselling the Intellectually Gifted Child

the *g* factor in intelligence, was the basis for the well-known matrix intelligence test. Thurstone's factorial theory led to the construction of special tests measuring such different abilities as verbal fluency (V) and numerical reasoning (N).

Guilford's theories of the structure of the mental intellect produced more than sixty kinds of intelligence tests. And of course, there are many others. Intelligence tests can be divided according to the kind of ability measured (verbal or performance), the conditions of administration (individual or group), or the age of the subject ("baby" tests, children's, or adults').

Two of the most widely-used intelligence tests for children in the Western world are the Binet test (with the Terman revision) and the revised edition of the Wechsler Intelligence Scale for Children, (WISC). The Binet test has not changed much from the form devised at the beginning of the century and most of the later tests have applied many of the principles introduced by Binet.

The WISC consists of twelve tests divided into two sub-groups, Verbal and Performance. Generally, to shorten the time required, examiners use only five Verbal and five Performance tests, and the I.Q. is calculated on this basis. The two tests usually omitted are Digit Span in the Verbal section and Mazes in the Performance section.

A look at the Verbal part of the WISC will help us to understand how and I.Q. score is made. The Verbal sub-tests of the WISC are the following (in this example, note that all six have been used).

1 *Information*: measures the breadth of one's accumulated knowledge. It includes questions such as "What is the capital of Holland?"

2 *Comprehension*: measures, among other things, knowledge of social norms and their comprehension. It includes questions such as "What do you do if you lose a toy belonging to a friend?"

3 *Arithmetic*: measures the capacity of dealing with mathematical problems. It includes such questions as, "If three children each received 20¢, how much will they have all together?"

4 *Similarities*: measures capacity for abstraction. In this sub-test the child is asked to explain what is common between two things such as "mouse" and "cat."

5 *Vocabulary*: measures knowledge of words. The child is asked to define such words as "temperature."

6 *Digit span*: measures attention and short-term memory. Here the child is asked to repeat digits which are read aloud to him.

The I.Q.'s on the WISC are obtained by comparing the child's score in each sub-test with the scores of individuals in a single age group – *his* age group – rather than with the performance of a composite age group. The total of the scores on the sub-tests give the verbal I.Q. of the tested child. Figure 2 illustrates the sub-test scores of three children each having an I.Q. of exactly 100. As we can see, their intellectual abilities are far from being equal. While child A has the same performance on all the sub-tests, the scores of B and C show some strong and some weak points in the different mental abilities. No conscientious counsellor will consider a general I.Q. score without looking into "how it is made up." This problem is less important with gifted children, since, in order to have a general I.Q. of 130, one has to be superior in all of the sub-tests. However, even with gifted children, some variability in the sub-tests scores does exist. Awareness and evaluation of this fact is very important for the guidance counsellor who deals with the gifted.

Since intelligence tests of many types and great variety are used to identify and measure intellectual abilities, it is worth while asking how well, in fact, they accomplish their purpose. How effectively do they reveal the *how much?* An unqualified answer is risky.

Fig. 2   THREE I.Q.S OF 100 ON THE VERBAL PART OF THE WISC

	80	90	100	110	120
Information	B		A		C
Comprehension	B		A		C
Arithmetic	B	C	A		
Similarities			A	C	B
Vocabulary	C		A		B
Digit Span	C		A		B

Obviously these three children all having an average I.Q. of 100, have very different mental abilities. Child A has scores of 100 on all sub-tests. Child B has low scores on the Information, Comprehension, and Arithmetic sub-tests, but high scores on Similarities, Vocabulary, and Digit Span. Child C has high scores on Information, Comprehension, and Similarities and low scores on Arithmetic, Vocabulary, and Digit Span. All sub-tests have different psychological meaning, and in order to understand each child's intellectual potential, the sub-test scores have to be understood, because the picture is more complex than it would appear by looking at the *average* I.Q. which is identical for all three children.

Counselling the Intellectually Gifted Child

In the last few years, especially in the United States, intelligence tests have come under severe criticism. It is appropriate now for us to discuss and evaluate these criticisms, and we shall conclude this chapter by giving the reader our own interpretation of the validity and utility of intelligence tests. First, what are the most common criticisms?

1 *The tests are of doubtful validity as predictors.* This argument boils down to the proposition that intelligence is a many-faceted, even mysterious matter, and that no test devised by humans can plumb the mystery. It follows that since the tests cannot get at the "true" meaning of intelligence, a prediction about the future of someone with a particular test score is an impossibility.

2 *The tests are misused scandalously by counsellors, personnel officials, teachers, administrators, and psychologists.* The argument is that users of tests generalize well beyond the data and claim too much for a particular score, and that the test scores are used unfairly as a basis for decisions about promotions, acceptance to college, and so on. It follows then that any test that is misused so abominably must be thrown out.

3 *The tests are culturally unfair.* It is believed that intelligence tests discriminate against members of certain minorities and against lower-class children. The scores of such segments of the community as those who speak a different language or who are new immigrants from poor environments, are statistically lower than the scores of the white, middle-class members of the majority. Therefore, the tests are culturally biased and ought not to be used.

4 *The tests are limited and do not measure divergent thinking or creativity.* Since, it is held, intelligence tests simply cannot deal with creative abilities or the ability to think, they are obviously too limited. They can tell us nothing important about intelligence and, therefore, are useless.

These objections should be answered. The answer can be based on a good deal of evidence, of many kinds, which has accumulated over the last decade.

First, how well do intelligence tests predict? The question should be rather, *what* do intelligence tests predict? They predict success in academic work. This is why they were designed originally. Those who score well in intelligence tests, in fact, tend to do well in academic work; of this there is little doubt. The correlation between I.Q. and academic achievement varies between .68 and .90 depending on the age of the subjects tested.[8] No other psychological measure can boast such a high correlation with an external criterion.

Do they predict success in business or marital adjustment? Do they tell one who is likely to be an effective manager, a productive scientist? Certainly not, and they were never designed to do this. There is no point in going beyond what the tests were designed to do, nor is there any point in arguing that they do not predict Nobel or Pulitzer Prize winners. Academic success, however, which the tests were designed to predict, is a very good indication of professional choices, as shown in Francis Steward's study. She analyzed the intelligence scores of 81,533 enlisted men in the American armed forces who were given intelligence tests during the Second World War. The results showed a clear relationship between the test results and the occupational level.[9]

Next, should we reject tests because the users misuse them? X-rays and encephalograms are misused by incompetent physicians. Must we then give up both diagnostic tools? This is a silly question; one should ask instead, "Why not train physicians to use the tools properly?" Similarly, if psychologists and others misinterpret intelligence-test data, the solution is not to throw out the instruments but rather, somehow, to see that potential users are trained more adequately. Those who understand intelligence testing, know that (1) an I.Q. is a composite score of sub-tests (see examples on page 16), and one should look into the meaning of each sub-test score; and (2) the reliability of an intelligence test is, in part, a function of time. A test given twice the same day has a correlation of .94, but, in a ten-year interval, the correlation is about .50.[10] Therefore, using the result of a test to put a child in a pigeonhole or to classify him for life is done only by those who entertain a superstitious belief in the "permanency" of I.Q.'s

Third, do tests discriminate unfairly against minorities? Sometimes they do: there is no doubt that only a very unintelligent test-giver would give an English verbal intelligence test to a Spanish-speaking child. Some researchers who believed that intelligence tests were unfair, tried to construct culture-free tests. The results of one such test,[11] did not change the fact that significant differences continued to exist beween groups, even on these tests. As we said, intelligence tests predict academic achievement and academic success is certainly not culture-free. One might as well argue that a weighing scale discriminates against those who suffer from malnutrition. If intelligence tests do – and they do – yield statistically different scores as between middle-class white and lower-class minority children, the solution is not to abandon the tests. The solution (if "solution" is the appropriate term), is to enquire into the reasons for the difference in scores. If the difference in scores has to do with poverty, child-raising patterns, poor nutrition, blatant social discrimination, and wretched housing, what is the point of criticizing intelligence tests and test scores? The

Counselling the Intellectually Gifted Child

test scores do reveal differences, and these differences are probably related to certain environmental factors. To discard the tests on this account is to attempt to provide the solution for another completely different problem.

Fourth, do tests measure divergent thinking? No, they probably do not, just as they do not measure creativity – whatever "creativity" may be. It is, however, by no means clear that creativity can be measured; at least creativity tests so far have not done so to any obvious extent. In spite of the current enthusiasm for creativity tests, research does not show that high scores on the tests predict anything at all. The so-called creativity tests, which more appropriately should be called divergence tests, are certainly promising instruments but more research is needed before they should be accepted as having any predictive value. The famous, and often criticised, Getzel and Jackson study showed that there were differences between children having high scores on creativity tests and those having high I.Q.'s[12] It should be remembered that both groups came from a population having a mean I.Q. of 130. When the same tests are given to a normal population, the correlation between the two tests is as high as .88[13]

The main trouble with creativity tests is that the only sure thing one can say about a child who has a high score on such a tests is that "he has a high score on such a test." When more validity is proven for creativity testing – a property they lack entirely[14] – they could be used with intelligence tests to give a better understanding of the intellectual process as a whole. While intelligence tests perhaps, are not a reliable measure of divergent thinking, they do fulfill their true function of distinguishing convergent thinking, the kind of thinking which is associated mainly with academic work. As we indicated before, this is what they were designed to do.

The conclusion must be, therefore, that I.Q. tests have a valid use in the determination of intelligence and, hence, of intellectual giftedness. Those who obtain very high scores on intelligence tests are those who justifiably may be termed "the intellectually able." Those who obtain high scores have good memories, have an impressive fund of information, reason clearly, and solve problems accurately. These characteristics may not be all there are to intellectual giftedness, but they are quite a lot.

Intelligence tests, used conservatively and with an appreciation of the limitations, are a valuable tool in the diagnosis of who is and who is not intellectually gifted. Over the years, the custom of labelling children who score in the top 3 per cent in intelligence tests as intellectually gifted, has much that is commendable. This judgement may have to be modified, or even discarded, in the future. But, for now, as we intend to use the term in this book, intellectual giftedness is the same as a very high intelligence; and by diagnosing intellectual abilities of a high order, intelligence tests have proven their worth. Of course, defining giftedness as the upper 3 per cent range in an I.Q. test is only the starting point. Other tests can, and should, be used in order to gain a better understanding of the processes underlying giftedness, such as motivation, emotional aspects, and creativity. By now, in spite of some existing criticism, this approach to giftedness is well accepted. The following chapter will survey the first systematic attempt at identifying giftedness in children and evaluate some of the major findings and conclusions.

The monumental work of Lewis Terman and his co-workers on the study of giftedness constitutes a true milestone in psychological study. Terman was the first person to use the scientific approach in comparative and longitudinal studies of the gifted. More than fifty years have passed since his original study, and still no serious writer reflects upon characteristics of the gifted without some reference to Terman's work. His research led to the discarding of some popular stereotypes about "negative" traits of gifted children and to the emergence of a new image of them as superior to the "average" child. The conclusions of Terman and his colleagues are forbiddingly lengthy, and it appears that many people are more acquainted with short resumés which are, at times, misleading, than with the full report. A careful overview of the whole study may illuminate some of the methodological problems which are not easily discernible and which may modify some of the generalizations usually applied to the gifted.

The Terman study, *Genetic Studies of Genius*, was published in five volumes between the years 1925 and 1959. The first volume was entitled *Mental and Physical Traits of a Thousand Gifted Children*. We shall review this volume rather extensively, because it is here that Terman presents characteristics of the gifted children. Volume II was a separate study by Catherine M. Cox, titled *The Early Mental Traits of Three Hundred Geniuses* (1926). Volume III, *The Promise of Youth* (1930), Volume IV, *The Gifted Child Grows Up* (1947), and the last volume, *The Gifted Group at Mid-Life* (1959), were follow-up studies of some of the gifted people in the original sample.

Terman began his ambitious project with a two-fold purpose. First, he wanted to find out what traits characterize children of extremely high I.Q. Second, he wished to follow them for as many years as possible to see what kind of adults they might become. The fulfillment of Terman's "dream" as he called his project, was made possible in the spring of 1921 by a grant from the Commonwealth Fund of New York City for the purpose of locating 1,000 subjects with an I.Q. of 140 or higher. With the help of four field assistants he canvassed a school population of nearly one quarter of a million in the urban and semi-urban areas of California. From this population, a total of 684 children with an I.Q. higher than 132 was selected, and was named the "main group." The children in the group underwent a variety of measurements, including physical measurements, medical examinations, and tests in achievement, character, and interests. Additional information was obtained from parents and teachers. A second group of 309 high school pupils with similar I.Q.'s was studied but not all the measurements previously mentioned were applied to this group. Additional information was obtained from parents and teachers.

The principal findings upon which Terman based on his main group of 684 gifted pupils may be summarized as follows:

1 Socio-economic Background

As a group, the children came from much higher socio-economic strata than did the children with average intelligence. Among the factors considered were: mean schooling of both parents (which was four grades more than the average American of that time), occupational background of the fathers (professional and semi-professional yielded 80 per cent of the gifted), and numbers of books in the home (more than 500 books in the homes of 1 out of 6 gifted).

2 Ethnic Origin

Children from white, English, Scottish, and Jewish background were over-represented in the sample of the gifted, while children from non-white and southern European families were under-represented.

3 Anthropometric Differences

Physically, as determined by various anthropometric measurements, the average height and weight of children in the gifted group was above the highest standards for American-born children at that time.[1]

4 Medical History

Terman found that the record of illness and physical injury of the gifted was not significantly different from that of average children. The single medical difference was that twice as many gifted children wore glasses.

5 School Achievements and Special Academic Abilities

The outstanding characteristic of the gifted was their educational precocity, as shown among other things, by the facts that 10 per cent of the gifted were accelerated in Grade 1 and that nearly 50 per cent learned to read before they started school.

With regard to special abilities in school, the superiority of the gifted over the unselected children was found to be greatest in reading,

Counselling the Intellectually Gifted Child

arithmetical reasoning, and information. There were no significant differences between the two groups in spelling, computation, and art information.

6 *Interest in Reading and other Activities*

The average gifted child was found to read 10 books in two months at age 7, and 15 books at age 11, with little increase afterwards. In the control group, only a few of those aged 8 or younger read any book; after 8, these children read fewer than half the number of books read by the gifted group.

In the field of games, plays, and amusements, the gifted children showed a preference for quiet, mildly social activities which required thought. Their interest in competitive activities was slightly less than that of the control group.[2] The gifted children preferred to play more mature games; they tended to play alone slightly more than the other children and to favour playmates who were slightly older.

7 *Sociability*

There was no significant difference in the ability of the gifted children to make friends in school although there was a slight tendency to their being regarded as "queer" or "different."[3]

8 *Character and Personality Traits*

On the basis of tests which measure many of the variables we would include today in the category of moral judgement, the gifted children were found to be superior. Ratings by teachers and parents showed the gifted children were superior in the following areas: intellectual, vocational, emotional, moral, physical, and social. Mechanical ingenuity was the only trait on which the control group was found to be higher.

In conclusion, Terman's findings showed that gifted children are significantly different and above the average child in socio-economic background, physical development, school achievement, reading ability, and personality traits.

Terman continued the study by following his subjects for thirty years. On the basis of a specially devised and difficult intelligence test, he found that the average scores of the gifted adult were as high above those of the general population as the scores that they had received as children. This prompted Terman to reject the popular maxim of "Early ripe, early rot" and to declare that no one of the people in his sample had developed post-adolescent stupidity."[4] These follow-up studies also convinced Terman beyond question, of the value of the administration of "general intelligence" tests at a young age and of their validity in the prediction of future achievement.

High intelligence, as measured by an I.Q. test alone, is not sufficient by itself to account for outstanding achievement. One of Terman's greatest contributions is that he brought to light the other factors which are necessary as well. In order to determine the factors contributing to success in adulthood, he investigated differences between the "successful" and "unsuccessful" gifted in his sample. The criterion of "success" was defined as "the extent to which a subject had made use of his superior intellectual ability." Ratings of success were made by three independent judges. Two groups, each of 150 men, were formed, one of the "successful" (called A) and of the "unsuccessful" (called C). The two groups were compared on two hundred items of information collected over almost twenty years. One of the important findings which emerged was that family background, and emotional and social adjustment are factors which strongly influence the realization of intellectual potential. It was discovered that the parents of group A had enjoyed a higher educational and occupational status. Three times as many C's as A's had been judged as children to have problems in emotional adjustment and to exhibit some kind of "nervous symptoms." From the point of view of social relationships, leadership was found to have been already higher in group A in childhood.

The importance of Terman's conclusions lies in his discovery that not only do factors other than intelligence play an important part in giftedness, but also that some of these factors are already discernible in childhood. Contrary to the popular belief that high achievement is related to maladjustment, Terman's study is also notable for having shown that "success is associated with stability rather than instability, with absence rather than presence of disturbing conflicts, in short, with well-balanced temperament and with freedom from excessive frustration."[5]

Terman himself, was aware of the possibility of errors and shortcomings in his pioneer effort to investigate the gifted. He believed that the true value of his work would be assessed by the extent to which it inspired others to undertake further research on the gifted. Unlike those psychologists who try to defend the supreme perfection of their findings, Terman asked for continual criticism and repeated investigations. Accordingly, we are offering some critical remarks about aspects of Terman's methodology and an evaluation of some of his instruments and conclusions.

First of all, the methodology of Terman's study involves some serious problems in the sampling itself. Terman's sample was constructed using teacher nominations as the first step. Children nominated by their teachers as intelligent were given intelligence tests and only those with IQ's above 132 were kept in the sample. However, the teacher-nomination procedure has been shown to be misleading. For instance, Jacobs showed that fewer than 10 per cent of the gifted children in kindergarten were nominated correctly by their teachers.[6] In primary school, teacher nomination missed about 50 per cent of the gifted.[7] It appears that teachers tend to consider as most intelligent those who receive the best grades. This procedure is almost guaranteed to miss gifted underachievers.

Another problem in Terman's sampling procedure is that he did not look for gifted children in the entire school population. In a critique of Terman's study, Hughes and Converse calculated that statistically Terman should have located 3,358 gifted children from the population he used instead of 684.[8] Terman, apparently, missed 2,674 children, almost four times the number in his sample. By looking in "good," i.e., upper socio-economic schools, Terman may have missed gifted children in the population as a whole. The result of this omission on Terman's part may mean that the most important characteristics of the gifted, as shown by Terman, may well be the effects more of socio-economic class differences than of degree of intellectual giftedness. There is enough evidence about the better physical status and better health of children from higher socio-economic classes; the reason for these differences is obvious. Since Terman did not compare the socio-economic background of his control group with that of his sample group of gifted children, and since in Terman's own terms, disproportionately more parents whose children are gifted come from higher socio-economic levels, the better physical traits of the gifted sample should not be surprising. In a study comparing a group of gifted children with their siblings, having an I.Q. at least 20 points lower, no differences were found in the physical and anthropometric measures used.[9] The study's conclusion was that, when socio-economic differences are controlled, the gifted child is not superior on physical variables. The only significant differences between the two groups were related to intellectual factors and some forms of behaviour. In his comparison of children with a mean I.Q. of 133.2 from the upper socio-economic level with youngsters with a mean I.Q. of 132.1 from the lower socio-economic level, Frierson found that the upper-status gifted had more positive attitudes toward school and read more than the gifted from the lower status.[10]

There is a possibility that one might reach different conclusions about the general characteristics of the gifted if one were to include gifted underachievers and gifted children from lower socio-economic levels in the gifted sample.

Additional criticism levelled at Terman concerns the instruments Terman used, since many of them seemed to be of doubtful validity. The fact that most of the personality and character tests he employed have disappeared from the psychologist's arsenal would suggest that they were indeed, of dubious value.

One may speculate on the "Rosenthal effect" in the questionnaires that Terman gave to teachers and parents. In 1966 Rosenthal showed that when teachers are told that their pupils have very high intellectual potential – even when the information given to teachers is manufactured for that purpose – their entire attitude towards these pupils becomes more favourable and the children receive better grades. It is very possible that this phenomenon in some way influenced the results of the Terman study, since the parents and teachers knew that the questionnaires dealt with gifted children.

Our own conviction is that, despite all of the data gathered, a strong aura of impersonality pervades the entire study. Questionnaires were used extensively, and there are very few instances of a personal interest in an individual child. It is remarkable that not a single child was ever observed in a play situation; if he was, it was not reported. What one finds is play interest investigated with such test questions as "'Throwing in the sponge' is a term used in Boxing/Horse Racing/Wrestling.'"[11] One wonders if there aren't better ways of investigating children's play.

In spite of these criticisms, there is no doubt that Terman's study constitutes the first, the most basic, and the most complete study of the gifted ever conducted. It may be true that Terman made serious errors in his procedures. It also remains true that the large amount of research done subsequently on the subject, essentially repeated his methods and validated most of his major conclusions. In the field of psychology, this is quite a rare accomplishment, and many a psychologist still stresses the uniqueness of such a feat. Terman's study gave impetus to further research in the field and fostered the large number of studies and investigations. It has been pointed out, however, that "the profusion of studies on giftedness was not matched by a profusion of findings . . . numerous investigations continue to discover and rediscover, to state and restate, what has already been known for decades."[12]

While we do not intend to review all of the research on the gifted conducted since Terman, we should like to mention briefly three ques-

Counselling the Intellectually Gifted Child

tions investigated by various other researchers because they touch upon some essential elements in the conception of giftedness. First, what are the relative influences of heredity and environment on the gifted, the age-old nature-nurture question? Second, what distinguishes children with an extremely high i.q. from those gifted children with an i.q. around 130? Third, how do the gifted adults, those who have made outstanding contributions to society, develop and become the social asset they represent?

It is interesting to note that however old a question it may be, the nature-nurture controversy is as heated today as it always was. The first scientific investigation of the problem was made by Sir Francis Galton, who, in 1869, wrote a book entitled, *Hereditary Genius.* His conclusions are clear from the title, and many later scientists have followed Galton's views on the genetic value of genius. But there are probably a greater number of researchers who have written against the concept of hereditary intelligence. Erlenmeyer Kimling and Jarvick reviewed fifty-two research papers published in eight countries over a period of fifty years.[13] Their study examined the results of ninety-nine research groups as to the existing correlation between kinship and intelligence. Their conclusions can be summarized in the following table, which gives the median correlations from the different studies:

Unrelated people	.10
Adoptive parents/child	.20
Parent/child	.50
Siblings	.49
Fraternal twins	.53
Monozygotic twins reared apart	.35
Monozygotic twins reared together	.87

This study shows the importance of heredity as well as environment in the relationship between intelligence and kinship. The effect of heredity is shown by the fact that the closer the kinship, the higher is the correlation in intelligence. The effect of environment, on the other hand, is indicated by both higher correlations between adoptive parents and their adoptive children as opposed to unrelated people, and between monozygotic twins reared together as opposed to monozygotic twins reared apart.

Even though there is no doubt that both factors play a role and neither one, by itself, can account for intelligence, is it possible that the delicate balance between hereditary and environmental factors plays a different role for the high levels of intelligence? Terman in the first phases of his research, believed that heredity had greater importance than environment for the explanation of giftedness. In the research studies we know, all but one indicate that a much higher proportion of gifted children comes from the families of professionals. One author[14] believes that a greater proportion of gifted children should be found in families with a lower socio-economic background simply because their proportion in society is higher. However, evidence does not substantiate this egalitarian and democratic hope.

Whether the question of the relative importance of heredity and environment will ever be settled is, at present, doubtful. In the first place, there is the basic difficulty of defining unequivocally the terms of heredity and environment. Second, there is the problem of devising instruments which measure the effects of both. As additional data are gathered every year, the question becomes less settled. Therefore, up to now, the question of the relative importance of heredity and environment is unanswerable. This is as true for the gifted as for the general population.

For the answer to our second question, "What distinguishes children with an extremely high I.Q.?" we turn to research conducted by Leta Hollingsworth in the 1930's and 1940's.[15] Hollingsworth located and studied twelve children with an I.Q. of 180 and higher. Children of this level of intelligence are hard to find; perhaps one or two with I.Q.'s of 180 occur in about one million. In spite of the limited sample and although she died before completing the description and analysis of her research, some valid conclusions may be reached.

What characteristics do these rare children share? It was found that they tend to be first-born. Ten of the twelve children in the sample were first-born and five of them were only children. To no one's surprise, all were marked by a great precocity; the median age for talking was fourteen months and for reading, thirty-six months. But many of the children in Hollingsworth's group experienced social difficulties. Hollingsworth thought later that the earlier the children were identified as extremely gifted, the fewer problems they would experience in the future. In the case of the Hollingsworth children, any simple generalization to the effect that "the more the better," or that the higher the I.Q., the better off a person is, is not tenable. Many of these extremely bright children did not make successful social adjustments or prove later to be exceptionally productive. In neither case are the reasons clear. The gifted children studied by Terman did well, as history has demonstrated, and the super-gifted did not do proportionately better. As we have said before, giftedness in children is only a promise; the fulfilment of the promise depends upon a host of non-intellectual factors.

Our third question was: "How do the gifted adults, those who make outstanding contributions to society, develop and become the social asset they represent?" Anne Roe looked into that question and examined sixty-four of the most eminent scientists in the United States as selected by a panel of experts in each field of science.[16] She examined intensively their life history, family background, professional and recreational interests, intelligence, achievement, personality, and ways of thinking – anything, in fact, which might have a bearing on the person's choice of his vocation and his success in it. Two main points of her study stand out:

1 There are some common characteristics for the whole group of scientists.
2 There are some differences which characterize the scientists in their particular field as a group.

The common characteristics of all the scientists were placed by Anne Roe in a profile which she called "the average eminent scientist." She found that he was the oldest child of a middle-class professional man with a very high I.Q. He may have been sickly as a child or have lost a parent at an early age. He had a tendency to feel lonely or shy and began to read extensively when very young. At a relatively late age, when he was already in college, he decided to become a scientist, a decision usually based on a college project which gave him the opportunity to do independent research in science. Once he realized the advantages of working on his own, he never regretted his choice of profession. His work is his life, and he has neither the time nor the inclination to pursue hobbies or an active social life. His non-working hours are spent with his family or in recreational pursuits which he can do by himself. He usually married late and finds security in family life; his marriage is usually more stable than the average.

Of course there are variations; this is a picture of the majority of the group studied. Some differences were simply individual; others were characteristic of the scientists in different fields. The latter are summarized in Figure 3 (page 30).

A summary of Roe's findings reveals that the striking points shared by all the scientists are high intelligence, independence, non-conformism, self-assertiveness, and a total and driving absorption in their work. These are the qualities that MacKinnon also found in a similar study in which he used as subjects, creative writers, architects, mathematicians, and research workers.[17] Barron did a similar study in 1969,[18] and his findings were similar to those of Roe. All the studies showed that intelligence is indispensable, but insufficient in itself to account for high achievement in any field. As Terman has already noted, other factors, such as special interests, perseverance, and high motivation, are most important in the achievement and creative processes.

Fig. 3   CHARACTERISTICS OF EMINENT SCIENTISTS IN DIFFERENT FIELDS

(adapted from Anne Roe)

	INTELLECTUAL ABILITIES	Personality characteristics based on		
		THEMATIC APPERCEPTION TEST	ROHRSCHACH TEST	SOCIAL RELATIONS
Social scientists	Spatial mathematics			
Experimental psychologists, Other psychologists, Anthropologists	Verbal	Rebellious, aggressive concern over inter-personal relations	Concerned with human beings	Intense social activity
Biologists, Geneticists, Biochemists	Verbal and non-verbal	More factual, less interested in feelings, unwilling to commit themselves	Concerned with forms	Shy, lonely, over-intellectual
Physical scientists	Verbal and spatial	Same as above but to a lesser extent	Concerned with space, inanimate things	Same as above

Counselling the Intellectually Gifted Child

But what is the nature of the creative process, or what is creativity? According to Guilford,[19] the salient feature of the creative process is divergent thinking, as opposed to convergent thinking. Guilford was the first to distinguish between these two types of thought processes. He defined convergent thinking as a situation in which one, and only one, possible solution exists for a given problem. For example, the question "How much is two and two?" requires but one answer. Divergent thinking, on the other hand, describes a situation in which two, three, or a great many answers or solutions are possible. Finding a title for a story may have many valid solutions. Interest in the divergent kind of thinking arose out of the dissatisfaction with the intelligence tests and their emphasis on convergent thinking. Divergent thinking became equated with creativity and many researchers, following the lead established by Guilford, became interested in the subject. Tests for measuring creativity were devised by the score and papers on the subject published by the thousands. By the mid-1950's creativity had moved almost to the status of a fad.

Two important questions resulted from the research on creativity:

1 What do creativity tests predict?

2 What is the relation between creativity and intelligence?

The answer to the first question is that the results are not very encouraging. In her excellent paper entitled *Creativity Tests: Boon or Boondoggle for Education*, S. B. Crockenberg reviewed research on the topic and concluded that high scores on creativity tests do not predict what others, qualified to judge, were able to call creativity.[20] George Erickson attempted to validate the work done by Paul Torrance, one of the main researchers in the field of creativity, and to verify that the subsequent achievement of students could be correlated with their scores on creativity tests. He reported positive and significant correlations.[21] Crockenberg reviewed Erickson's reports and concluded that in view of the criteria of the creative achievements, the correlations should not be regarded as especially significant.[22] The creativity criteria quoted by Erickson included subscriptions to professional magazines, changes of religious affiliation, election to a student office, and learning a new language.

As for the relation between intelligence and creativity, it seems that correlations between the two decrease in size as the i.q. increases. In other words, in the lower and normal ranges of intelligence, creativity and intelligence tests measure more or less the same phenomena, so that at these levels of intelligence the correlation between the two is low. At superior levels of intelligence the correlation between the two is high. High intelligence does not imply the possession of high creativity, but it seems clear that high intelligence is basic and essential for outstanding achievement. Better creativity tests could perhaps be devised, and they should include tests for the presence of other variables which are determinants of creativity. However, more data is necessary. The interested reader is advised to consult the extensive literature on the subject, the best of which is probably Hudson's *Contrary Imaginations*.

This rapid overview of a half century of research on the gifted has emphasized the conclusions of the Terman study. The study is a landmark which represents the turning point from the equating of giftedness to genius, maladjustment, and insanity to scientific investigation and the search for empirical evidence to describe and explain its characteristics. One generalization emerges from the studies reviewed in this chapter: the promise that lies in high intelligence, in itself, does not ensure high achievement. Some highly intelligent children will eventually make a contribution to society; many others will not, for many non-intellective factors affect the full realization of high intelligence.

Competent counsellors with the help of parents and teachers can play an essential role in contributing to the fulfillment of the promise inherent in high intelligence. In this role the counsellor will have to keep in mind not only the special characteristics the gifted child shares with other gifted children, but also the unique and distinctive characteristics that make him an individual in his own right. The next chapter deals with some of the characteristics of the gifted child.

4   Characteristics of the Intellectually Gifted Child

Saul is a nine-year-old boy who just now is bored by the way his playmates are playing marbles. After a little thought he decides that marbles would be more interesting if the traditional rules and procedures were modified. Accordingly, he invents his own version of the game. But when he explains his bright new idea to his friends, Saul finds that some are reluctant to try his way; some simply don't understand his explanation, and others cast perplexed looks at him and decide that they would rather play with someone else. Saul is a bit upset but before long, he begins to look for others who will be more receptive to his new marble game. The boy has difficulty in finding anybody who is interested. Finally, he collars his brother who is twelve, and explains the invention to him. Benny listens attentively, agrees that the new version is worth a try, and takes Saul to meet his gang. The gang listens, approves, experiments, and decides to adopt Saul's rules for the game and, in addition, Saul himself. Saul's happiness is short-lived, however, for once the older boys in the gang tire of the new marble game, they discover that Saul cannot keep up with them in their other activities. Saul not only lacks their physical skills, but he is naive where they are sophisticated and hesitant where they are self-confident. The older boys decide to drop Saul because, as the gang tells Benny, "He's just a kid."

Michael, aged twelve, is conspicuously bored with his classes, his teachers, his books, and, ultimately with himself. One alert teacher notes Michael's lack of interest and suggests that the boy read and think about one of the novels of Dostoyevsky, a work that is well beyond his classmates. Michael reads it, compares it with a novel by Victor Hugo, and then presents a long report to the class on "The Development of the Tragic Figure in Nineteenth-Century Romantic Novels." But there are no other teachers who are sensitive to Michael's needs and after finishing this project, he again becomes bored by school. He hears that the local university is offering a mathematics and computer-science course for high school children; he investigates and decides to sign up. Michael's interest in mathematics is not particularly in deep – certainly not as keen as his interest in literature – but there are no opportunities for him to receive further guidance and assistance in literature. Because of this, Michael chooses science and mathematics as his majors in high school. He performs well and, in addition, continues to read serious literature on his own. But others who are now aware of Michael begin to wonder silently if the world has not lost a writer or a future literary critic. So, occasionally, does Michael.

At the age of fourteen, Naomi has discovered mathematics. She picks up a book on Boolean algebra and then another on probability theory. Her interest in mathematics grows, and so does her mother's anxiety. "Naomi, I wish you wouldn't slouch around in the house and read. You'll ruin your eyes. Why don't you go out and meet boys and girls your age?" Naomi, in an effort to end her mother's nagging, does try to make new friends. Since she is adequately attractive she is asked for a date by Rod. When the two are out together, Naomi babbles on about the possibilities inherent in calculus, and soon observes that Rod is peering at her uncomfortably. Naomi uses her intellectual gifts to analyze the situation. She concludes that boys do not like girls who are smarter than they, and decides that the best course is to become an "underground" mathematician. She continues to read in mathematics but, to prevent her mother from complaining too loudly, she also continues to date. Now everyone is happy because Naomi is more like the person girls her age "should be."

Mary is thirteen years old. She paints for a hobby, although with no special distinction, and has "trained" her parents to take her to all of the latest art exhibitions and gallery shows. Her father is a fair chess player and taught Mary the game when she was eleven. She now beats him in three out of five games; this leaves Daddy with ambivalent feelings. Mother takes Mary to the library two days a week. She buys her daughter three or four paperbacks at a time and Mary devours them in three days. She enjoys school and is enjoyed by her teachers and by her classmates who recognize Mary's intellectual attainments, but are neither jealous nor resentful. In ways other than her intellectual interests and achievements, she is not particularly distinguishable from other thirteen-year-old girls. She has few close friends and many acquaintances and goes on outings and excursions with them. She has highs and lows, although she is usually cheerful. Her room is a perpetual litter, which prompts her mother to lecture her and, occasionally, to punish her. Mary promises to do better but, in fact, has not. Mary enjoys teasing her fifteen-year-old brother occasionally and bossing her nine-year-old sister always.

These four biographical sketches realistically reflect some of the varieties of gifted young people. Although many (perhaps most) are, like Mary, well adjusted and happy, functioning well within home and school, many others are more like Saul, Michael, and Naomi. Some, like Saul, drift uneasily between the company of children their own age, with whom they are intellectually unequal, and that of older children with whom they are socially unequal. Some, like Michael, select a scholastic major or a vocation, not because they want it, but because they have no other viable option. In effect, their choice is constricted. Finally, there are those like Naomi who become "underground" mathematicians, poets, or social philosophers. They still function, after a fashion, but much like the gambler or alcoholic who practises his vice in secret.

The fact that it is extremely difficult to paint a clear, unified picture of those whom we call "the gifted" should not surprise us, for the gifted are as heterogeneous as any other segment of the population. Any attempt at description should be made cautiously, for within this population, there seems to be more difference and variabliity than resemblance. Hundreds of papers have been written about the gifted by psychologists, educators, and even parents, and we have a great deal of statistical evidence on the subject. It is erroneous however, to apply inferences from generalizations about a large number of children to one particular gifted child. Differences do exist among gifted children. But, *as a group*, gifted children are different in many significant ways from average children *as a group*.

While, as we have indicated, there is much that we do not know and much that is still in the realm of speculation, it would be inconceivable if, after almost three-quarters of a century of research on the subject, we could not make some statements with confidence. We have data in abundance, for instance, on how much and how fast gifted children learn.

A distinctive intellectual characteristic of the gifted is their mental precocity. Gifted children frequently learn to read before they enter school and this makes enormous quantities of knowledge available to them for exploration. Another conspicuous trait is the constant, pointed questioning of gifted children – to the frequent despair of parents and teachers. Speed of learning is yet another distinguishing characteristic. The accelerated development of language in gifted children, their use of more complex expressions, and a level of oral exchange much higher than that of other children their own age may explain why gifted children prefer interaction with older children or adults. Flanagan estimated that gifted children in high school learned twice as rapidly as others in subjects which were of particular interest to them.[1]

Many of the traits and characteristics of gifted children are readily observable in their everyday behaviour. Early indications of superior intelligence include curiosity, imagination, a keen sense of humour, a broad attention span, and unusual interests. Most of the researchers investigating the intellectual development of these children at both the primary and secondary school levels found that a retentive memory, voracious reading habits, and intellectual curiosity were characteristics of the gifted. These children showed these qualities early, allied with a large vocabulary and extensive information. They are highly motivated and demonstrate development of self-criticism, initiative, and originality at an unusually young age.

At the college level, a study was made comparing 918 National Merit Scholars, whose estimated mean I.Q. was 150, with 841 students from the University of California and the University of Michigan.[2] This work showed that the high intellectual aptitude of the gifted was reflected in a strong disposition towards abstract thinking, an interest in ideas and conceptualization, and in a rational cognitive approach to reality. Although National Merit Scholars are selected on the basis of tests which are of a convergent nature, they appeared to be more original in their ways of coping with the environment and showed a greater potential for creativity. This work highlights one of the most important facts concerning the nature of the high intellectual abilities of the gifted: they are continued throughout life.

Some children seem to be obsessed at an unusually early age with seeking and learning specific, varied subjects. For these children encyclopaedias are often the preferred reading material. To date, there has been no research on why some children interest themselves in, for example, mathematics, while others build impressive collections of fossils or rocks. It is not now known why a child may become so absorbed in aeronautics that he collects pictures of every variety of civilian and military aircraft and commits to memory the distinguishing characteristic of each model. We do know, however, that this is precisely what happens in some instances.

The reasons why some gifted children invest their interests in one specific field as opposed to any other have not yet been investigated. From our experience with gifted children, however, we believe that most of them direct their intellectual inquiries towards subjects in which their parents are interested. This is certainly the case for most of the gifted children we know who have professional parents. Of course there are gifted children who discover, by and for themselves, areas about which their parents have little or no knowledge. It is these children who raise yet another question worthy of further investigation: are their explorations the result of teacher influence or of sheer accident? Despite the present dearth of information on this whole aspect of the subject, there is one fact of which we are certain; the gifted child's eagerness to learn is his most salient characteristic, whether or not his interests are directed toward the usual school curricula.

Even among children, particular intellectual traits seem to be associated with certain personality variables. D'Heurle studied 75 Grade

Three students who scored in the 90th percentile or above on national norms for intelligence and achievement, and he followed them through the ninth grade.[3] Using the Rorschach Test, observation, and the Children's Apperception Test, he studied correlations between personality variables and reading, arithmetic, and spelling achievement. He concluded that particular personality traits are related to particular areas of intellectual achievement. For instance, those children who were high achievers, as shown in all of the achievement tests administered, accepted adult values and were well-adjusted, sensitive, and responsive to social pressures. However, those who scored high in arithmetic achievement were found to be more spontaneous and creative, and more aggressive, independent, and self-confident. The high reading achievers were, by contrast, found to be withdrawn, insecure in their relations with adults, and somewhat negative in response to parental authority. Although their relations with others were more inhibited, their fantasies were rich. High spelling achievers seemed to be passive; it was judged that they sought approval from adult authorities by adhering strictly to rules.

In 1925, Lewis Terman found achievement of the gifted to be greatest in reading, language usage, arithmetical reasoning, and information in science, literature, and the arts.[4] It should be noted, however, that these intercorrelations tended to be higher for younger gifted children than for the adolescent gifted. We would suggest as a possible reason for the tendency, the inclination among the gifted during adolescence towards more preoccupation with one specific field. Investing more intellectual energy in one field means, obviously, that less energy is invested in others. As a result, specialization in a given area appears in the gifted during pre-adolescence. While this same phenomenon is observable in average children, its occurrence there is much less frequent.

In addition to the research investigating the relationship between ability and personality, work has been done recently to determine the relationship between ability and interests. Let us remember that among the abilities of the gifted measurable by intelligence tests are the degree of general intelligence, the ability to do abstract and relational thinking, the ability to generalize, and the ability to execute tasks of a high degree of difficulty. Bart found that in the areas of biology, history, and literature, there is little or no association between the level of interest and the level of formal reasoning or intelligence.[5]

In a previously discussed survey of eminent scientists and social scientists (Figure 3), two traits, and, apparently only two, stood out. All were considered intellectually able and all were hard-working, educated, and persistent scholars. However, the variety of intellectual and personality styles was singularly evident. Some scored high on tests of verbal ability, others were average. Different personality traits, for example, concern for interpersonal relations as against a tendency to be lonely, shy, and aloof, showed up upon analysis, as did environmental factors. If one then asks why it is possible to generalize about physicists, about psychologists, or about biologists, the answer is hard to find.

Do some children drift early into a particular intellectual field because they wish to invest more energy in one area than another? Are the interests and/or vocations of parents in some sense determinative? Is it possible that accident and circumstance are significant? That is, can one trace the entry of a person into, say, physics or anthropology, because a particularly charismatic instructor "got hold of him?"

The problem of how to account for the particular interest, drive, or developed capacity of the gifted remains, after any amount of analysis, a problem. That the gifted are highly intelligent is a simple statistical phenomenon, demonstrated by decades of research and testing. That those gifted who succeed in becoming eminent scientists are tenacious, driving, intense workers is also largely true.[6] But when we ask: How did they get that way? or: Through what combination – if indeed it is a combination nature-nurture problem – of inherited traits and environmental circumstances do some people become physicists, some mathematicians, some art historians, and others inventors, the answer is, at present, most unclear. One thing is apparent, however; those who have the responsibility of teaching and counselling gifted young people have a very heavy responsibility indeed.

Alert readers may be curious or even annoyed about the absence of material on the artistically gifted in this work. We began, please recall, by deliberately limiting the scope of this book to the *intellectually* gifted. This does not mean that we are indifferent to other forms of giftedness. It is simply that very little that is scientifically valid has been unearthed about those who manifest talent in the arts and music. Musicians, composers, painters, and sculptors tend to manifest their abilities early. There is no very clear association between artistic skills and intellectual abilities, and, beyond this, we do not seem to know much that we deem reliable. The interested reader should consult Barron's *Artists in the Making*[7] which is concerned with visual art, actors, dancers, and writers.

From a counsellor's point of view, the contents of this chapter may seem depressing and not a little frustrating. The counsellor asks: What should I tell the gifted child and how can I counsel him into the right field? These, unfortunately, are not the right questions. Given the abundant confusion about interests, intellectual traits, and the

Counselling the Intellectually Gifted Child

capacities of gifted children, the counsellor's job is not *directive*. There is no reason for counsellors to direct gifted youngster F into field Z. The counsellor's task, rather, is the complex one of assisting the gifted child to clarify for himself not only his own capacities and interests, but also his values, desires, and preferences. The counsellor cannot like Moses, point the way to the promised land. He can only provide a map with which the gifted youngster can decide which, if any, is *his* promised land.

II

»The Counsellor and the Gifted Student«

5   Problems of the Gifted

The same wide range of problems is found among gifted children as among average children. Some problems, however, stem specifically from their giftedness. This chapter will deal with two such problems: underachievement and social relations.

Underachievement

Paramount among the problems of the intellectually gifted is the problem of underachievement, a phenomenon identifiable in all schools and at all academic levels. It is important to clarify at the beginning what we mean by the term, because it is one which has been juggled with extensively in professional literature, each time with a different result. To begin with, underachievemnt is a theoretical psychological term created to label an observable phenomenon. As we have noted, intelligence tests are highly correlated with school achievement, and one can predict fairly well the school grades to be received by children when we know their I.Q. The prediction is not wholly accurate, however, and discrepancies between I.Q. and school grades do exist. These discrepancies form the basis for a definition of underachievement. When a child with a high I.Q. has low grades in school, he is described as an "underachiever"; when he has a medium I.Q. and very high grades, he is considered an "overachiever." Since our society values achievement highly, overachievement is encouraged and there has been very little effort to investigate it systematically.

Underachievement, on the other hand, has provoked a great deal of interest. Literally hundreds of papers and articles written during the 1950's and 1960's presented a multitude of possible causes of underachievement and yielded contradictory conclusions; this total lack of agreement led some to decry the whole subject as "blatant myth." They contended that an organism's behaviour is explainable through its many contributing elements, and so, given all the biological and social factors, every individual achieves what he can and does the best he can in the circumstances in which he finds himself. Others considered that the whole concept of underachievement was an artifact for two reasons. First, as underachievement is based on academic achievement (which in turn is reflected in the school grades), it is not only intellectual capacity which comes into question, but also a whole array of other variables, such as good behaviour, tidy habits, clean work, friendliness, and so on. Second, when a discrepancy occurs between the scores on an intelligence test and the school grades, it is quite possible that the school grades reflect the intelligence level better than the test scores.

But even if there is some truth in these points, the fact that for 70 to 80 per cent of the children, the school grades are well related to the I.Q. entitles one to ask why isn't this so for a minority of children? When two pupils have identical scores on the same intelligence test, one can expect approximately the same academic achievement. When one of these pupils does not produce as well as the other, one must be sure to ask why. Many a teacher or parent can reflect easily on the number of times he has caught himself saying "but he really could do better," thus using the concept of underachievement.

The exact definition of underachievement is largely a matter of dispute between authors. Some writers in their definition use the discrepancy between scores in intelligence tests and school grades; others use the discrepancy between intelligence test scores and achievement tests scores. Other writers express still different views. We believe that the important thing is the discrepancy which exists for some children between their potential and their actual achievement. Of course, this discrepancy is a reality, not only in school and academic tasks, but in every field of human endeavour where one can speak about a possible achievement level and a particular actual achievement. What one is able to do and what one is willing, prepared, and motivated to do (and is actually doing) are sometimes far apart. And if one achieves according to one's potential in a particular field one may be producing well below one's potential in another field.*

To return to the academic achievement of gifted children in the school environment, their main achievement, or so it looks to educators, is learning, and "good" learning should be reflected in good grades. There is nothing more provocative to teachers and parents alike as having an able youngster (high potential = I.Q. 130 or more) who refuses to do good work (intellectual achievement = high grades). If a youngster fails to attain the academic excellence which his outstanding ability suggests he can attain, he is an underachiever. Two elements enter into an operational definition of the term: his I.Q. and his grades. Our working definition then for underachievement is: "functioning, as measured by grades, below one's potential, as measured by I.Q."

Why is understanding and evaluation of the gifted underachiever so important? We feel strongly that failure to thoroughly understand

---

*As an exercise in self-understanding the reader may try to think about the areas in which he is underachieving.

and evaluate the talent our society possesses now will gravely hamper the promise for the future. In our first chapter, we saw how the waste of intellectual potential constitutes a serious loss for society, but if such a recognition is important for society it is even more so for the child himself.

The child who is not recognized as a gifted underachiever starts off on the academic road developing a pattern of problems which place him in a vicious circle from which it will be hard for him to disentangle himself. The pattern begins by his learning not to learn, while others are developing study habits and skills for learning. He needs to make little, if any, effort to receive good grades, and this is precisely what he does. As he advances through the grades and academic tasks and demands become harder and he has to apply some effort, the underachiever does not know how. Up to now, good results have rewarded his lack of effort. He feels that it is simply not "elegant" to start applying himself now and that there is no magic in achieving good grades, if hard work is needed. At this point, the pattern of underachievement begins to pierce the youngster's defences. His self-esteem may drop, he may become disgusted with school and reject assignments *a priori*, and he may start to loathe anything that has to do with school. At the end of the school road he will be faced with doors to higher education which are closed to him. The whole process is self-defeating; the youngster is slowly killing within himself the very characteristics which make him so special: his thirst for knowledge, his insatiable curiosity, and his strong intellectual needs. Even if he decides that his one interest is a particular branch of science and that he will apply his unusual gifts to this field only, he will not be able to pursue the subject in university because his grades on the whole are low. Such an individual will experience an ever-nagging sense of personal failure.

Understanding the causes of underachievement should be the first logical step in the process of helping the underachiever. Unfortunately, research into the aetiology of underachievement is, for the time being, unable to present a clear picture, because the problem is extremely complex, and can be approached from very different points of view. Research always starts with a theory, so various writers will have varying *a priori* views about the connotative factors in underachievement. These, in turn, will influence their perspective on the problem. For example, the psychoanalysts' perspective is based on parental influence and the sociologist's on peer groups; the educational psychologist will look into the school curriculum.

Since a whole book could be devoted to a review of research findings concerning the aetiology of underachievement, we shall restrict ourselves to consideration of two aspects of possible causes of under-achievement, the Family and the School.

THE FAMILY

Many researchers see the parents and the home as the prime causes of underachievement. Some view the child as rebelling against the demands and attitudes of his parents; others see the child trying un-successfully to conform to their wishes and high expectations. We should emphasize that most psychologists who have investigated chil-dren's development agree implicitly with the *tabula rasa* concept, that the child's development is mainly the result of parental behaviour and attitude. It follows, therefore, that underachievement is viewed as being a direct result of parental attitudes. To us, however, it is obvious that children differ from one another at birth and that their reactions are not merely reactions to, but also individual and active ways of dealing with, their environment. Parents certainly influence children, but children, in turn, strongly influence their parents.

If, as we think, children's underachievement is a likely result of parental attitudes and behaviour, it is also wise to remember that underachievement may produce new forms of parental behaviour. In other words, the child, on discovery that he can influence his parents in many ways and that school achievement is important to them as it is to most parents in our society, may use his school grades to "reward" or "punish" his parents. The relationship between parental influence and children's underachievement is a two-way process; each can affect the other. We want to stress this point, since most re-searchers regard underachievement as a one-way process; they look into parental actions and try to understand from them how the child develops into an underachiever.

The easiest way to understand underachievement is to study ob-jective differences in the family situation of the underachievers as con-trasted with those of the achievers. Such objective-differences studies centre on such variables as family constellation, divorce rates, and socio-economic background. In 1970, Pringle investigated 100 gifted underachievers in England and found that 18 per cent of them com-pared to 6 per cent in the general population, had only one parent.[1] But the Talent Preservation Project, which studied 4,875 children in the United States did not find any significant differences in the family constellation of gifted underachievers.[2] Similarly, in Canada, McGilli-vray interviewed the parents of 100 gifted eighth-graders, among them achievers and underachievers.[3] He found no differences in the size of the family, the birth order, the number of broken homes, or the edu-cational level of parents. The only significant difference which Mc-

Counselling the Intellectually Gifted Child

Gillivray found was in the interest which the parents paid to their children's schooling; parents of achievers showed more interest in their children's school work than did parents of underachievers.

Some investigation has been done on the attitudes of fathers and mothers and their possible influence on their sons' and daughters' underachievement. Shaw compared parental attitudes towards independence training and their relation to academic achievement.[4] He found that fathers of underachieving boys were more concerned with their sons' social autonomy, and that a comparable concern was found in mothers of underachieving girls. Groth studied academic achievement of and parental influence on members of Mensa, the international organization whose members score in the upper two per cent on intelligence tests.[5] She found that high-achieving males need support from "warm" mothers during the first seven years of life; high-achieving females need support from both parents. Nichols, however, found the children of authoritarian mothers get better grades in school and more favourable ratings from their teachers.[6] As we can see, the findings are contradictory. One possible explanation may lie in the use of differing methodology. Each researcher devised his own instrument, and no exact replication of a published study has ever been made.

Another possible explanation of the confusion and ambiguity of research results may be the lack of very distinct patterns of underachievement. There are two well-defined populations of underachievers, the "bright" and the "gifted," and unambiguous results can only be arrived at by consistent differentiation between the two groups. The underachieving children described in the professional literature are from both groups, and tentative explanations are offered for their performance in school, which is lower than their I.Q. scores predict. However, the experiences and life situation of the bright underachiever (I.Q., 110–20) are distinctly different from those of the gifted underachiever (I.Q., 130 or over). The bright underachiever receives low grades which unequivocally push him in a precarious position. Teachers push him to achieve higher grades, upset and disappointed parents exert pressure on him, and his peers perceive him in a not-so-complimentary way. Obviously the psychological stress on the child is intense; the outcome is a transposition from one area of maladjustment to many others. There exists a plethora of literature concerning the child's suffering "self-esteem," his "neurotic syndrome," and many additional kinds of maladjustments, symptoms, and pathology resulting from his underachievement.

The story of the gifted underachiever is quite different; when one contrasts the two groups; something less obvious and less suspect operates. Very often the gifted underachiever remains unnoticed. He may possess an I.Q. of 140, but neither he, nor his parents, nor his teachers are aware of it. Thus when he brings home grades which are acceptable B's, no one worries or is upset. Consequently, he maintains the status quo and thereby sets in motion a strong pattern of under-achievement which all too often is discovered much later – often too late. The gifted underachiever therefore, could be labelled the "hidden" type, and many of the obvious and observable generalizations which are true for the bright underachiever are not true for him.

The author recently attempted to investigate the differences in self-concept between the bright and the gifted underachiever.[7] In this research, 67 gifted children with an I.Q. of 140 or over, were identified from a population of 2,000 children. This group of the gifted included 23 children whose school grades were in the lower 75 per cent of their class; these were the gifted underachievers. A second group of 61 children with I.Q.'s of 110–115, was identified from the population and divided into two sub-groups: those having above-average grades (the achievers and those whose grades were lower than average (the underachievers). Four new groups were formed from the original two groups:

1 Gifted achievers (I.Q., 140), academic achievement in the upper 90 per cent.

2 Gifted underachievers (I.Q., 140), academic achievement in the lower 75 per cent.

3 Bright achievers (I.Q., 110), academic achievement above average.

4 Bright underachievers (I.Q., 110), academic achievement in the lower 30 per cent.

A battery of tests was administered to the four groups of children and their parents, and the results were compared. It is important to note that both parents and children were tested since this procedure was helpful in understanding some of the parental influences on their children's patterns of underachievement.

One aspect of the research dealt with the self-image, which was measured using the semantic differential approach.[8] The test consisted of 18 pairs of adjectives presented in the following manner:

STRONG .... WEAK
SHY   .... OUTGOING
SLOW   .... QUICK

While the child was completing the semantic differential test, his parents completed the same scale. They were given the same list with the same instructions except that instead of being asked "how are

Counselling the Intellectually Gifted Child

you?" they were asked "how is your child?" Care was taken that each child and each parent completed the questionnaire without collaboration. Scores were computed separately for each child and for each parent. The differences in the self-image of the four groups of children studied appear in Figure 4. An analysis of variance was computed for the bright and the gifted groups, and significant differences were found among them. The bright achievers had a higher self-image than the bright underachievers but the reverse was true for the gifted group, that is, gifted underachievers were higher in self-image test scores than gifted achievers.

Fig. 4   SCORES OF SELF-IMAGE OF GIFTED AND BRIGHT CHILDREN

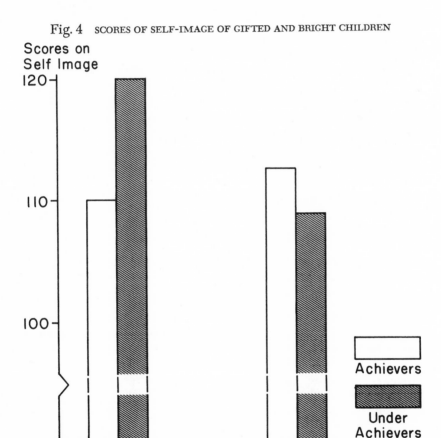

At first sight the results seem surprising. Is it not natural for achievers to feel better about themselves, with all the ego-boosting that comes with success? Indeed, among the bright pupils tested, this is precisely what was found. For the bright pupil, school work and the ensuing grades are his main avenues to success. It is in the school that he shows what he can do, and it is with his grades that he proves his superiority. But if his grades are low, if he fails, the blow to his self-esteem is tremendous and, in addition, he is reprimanded for his failure. There is no peace for the bright youngster who fails. He arouses everyone's concern or anger, and his self-image becomes as dark as the picture which others paint of him. For the gifted pupil, however, school is not the only way to success. His world is filled with the excitement and the thrill of discovery of an unlimited number of activities in different realms of life. Ego-boosting for him comes from many directions and not from school exclusively. His self-image reflects the excellence he develops in his favourite skills.

When we looked into the parents' views of their children as revealed by our study, here again significant differences appeared. While parents of the bright achievers evaluated their children in a more positive way than did parents of bright underachievers, the parents of gifted underachievers had a more positive view of their children than did those of gifted achievers. It seems that parents of a gifted underachiever appreciated and valued their child, not as a result of his work in school, but as a function of many other talents which a gifted child shows. We believe that the results of this research may help to formulate research hypotheses which could help bring about a better understanding of some of the underachieving patterns of the gifted child connected with the family relations.

THE SCHOOL

In general, the school pays little attention to the child who is out of tune with its usual expectations. The philosophy, objectives, and methodology of the school explicitly state that the orientation and focus are on the "average" child. The gifted child has two choices; he can revolt or he can hide his giftedness and become an average child, ending up as a gifted underachiever. One of the main causes of underachievement in a gifted child at school is related to the lack of challenge offered by the curriculum of the average school. Little David, whom we presented in the Introduction, is a typical example of a child in whom lack of challenge creates boredom and rejection. A keen, critical, gifted pupil may easily find himself in conflict with the teacher who does not understand him. Such conflicts between teacher and pupil can lead to punitive actions by the teacher and lack of motivation in the child. This sort of relationship can be the starting point of a pattern of underachievement. Such a pattern may be started early in the school life of a child. Once it has taken a firm hold, it is not easily changed. Shaw and McCuen showed that the onset of academic underachievement appears in boys in the third grade but in girls only in the 9th grade.[9]

Underachievement is related to sex differences, and all observers agree on one main fact: boys greatly outnumber girls. Underachievement is predominantly a male problem. A review of the studies which have explored this problem indicates that approximately half of all males who are above average in ability may be considered underachievers.[10] The corresponding figure for females is approximately 25 per cent. (A striking parallel can be seen in psychological clinics, where the number of boys referred for various problems is twice as high as the number of girls.)

Some causes for this phenomenon at the elementary level can be examined in the light of a factor inherent in our western educational establishment. We take it for granted because we are used to it, but it certainly may play an important role in the greater frequency of underachievement in boys at that level. We have labelled this aspect the "feminization of education." In a world where "feminization" usually points to problems of the human female, we know that it is not fashionable to talk about the difficulties of the human male. Everybody seems to be preoccupied with the underprivileged, exploited, and misunderstood situation of the female. By no means do we wish to deny the reality of this situation. We would, however, like to accentuate another facet of the relationship of sex differences and underachievement.

"Feminization of education" describes the fact that in our elementary schools the teaching profession has come increasingly into the hands of women in the last decade. From kindergarten through their elementary-school years, little boys live in a world where their teachers are women. It is more difficult for a boy than for a girl to identify with a woman and to respond to her expectations. One gifted boy who came to our clinic expressed the problem vividly. He was sent in to us because, although he had an I.Q. of 146, his grades were low. When we asked him if he found his school work difficult, he answered emphatically, "Oh, no, but very boring. The teacher pays attention to the neatness of our notebooks. She expects the pages to be decorated with flowers and curlicues of all colours." He added with contempt, "That's for girls; if you want to see what I'm good at, come during recess when I lead my gang into some wild stuff." This child was expressing his frustrations at the very real fact that for many boys, the expectations of female teachers are not as readily acceptable as they are for little girls. This very reaction may also be at the root of the fact that little boys like school less than little girls do – a fact universally detected.

The pattern of underachievement and its prevalence among boys changes in high school where there are more male teachers. At the high school level more underachieving behaviour is found among girls than among boys. But before the wrath of the feminist movement descends upon us, we should add that the feminization of education is but one factor in the predominance of underachievement among boys.

Underachievement as a whole is a very complex behaviour pattern, and anyone looking into its causes should take into consideration a great number of variables which might influence it. Since one of the important variables in school is the influence of the peer group, we shall examine next the important question of the social relations of the gifted.

Social Relations

Over the years, the social perception of the gifted child, has, like a swinging pendulum, alternated from one extreme to the other. Traditionally, the gifted child was seen as a lonely, isolated, maladjusted, and often unhappy creature. In recent years, by contrast, the gifted child has been shown as healthier, better adjusted, and more popular than the average child. We contend that neither picture is accurate; we believe that the older image of the gifted was distorted by negative stereotypes and that the happier picture of giftedness is inaccurate as well, because of methodological oversights. We believe that a more complete picture of the gifted would reveal both the positive and negative elements of the gifted child's characteristics.

We have already discussed the picture of gifted children drawn by Terman and his associates, a picture which was almost completely positive. Terman's gifted children were healthier than the average child, achieved well in school, knew more about sports, participated in more hobbies, and read more books. Terman's research does, however, give some inkling of not-quite-undisturbed social relationships of the gifted child. He was seen as slightly more "queer" or "different" than the others and as showing a slight preference for playing by himself.[11] But this is only a hint that all is not well. In general, Terman's children were much like average children, only more so. The researchers who followed Terman and used the same age groups, essentially repeated these findings.

However, when we leave Terman's interpretations and examine the conclusions of researchers who looked at gifted adults, a rather different picture emerges. We have already presented details from Anne Roe's study on scientists. She concluded that a composite picture of biologists and physicists showed characteristics of shyness, loneliness,

Counselling the Intellectually Gifted Child

and excessive intellectuality.[12] MacKinnon, who studied architects and writers, characterized their childhood and adolescence in similar terms.[13] Goertzel and Goertzel, in their book *Cradles of Eminence*,[14] examined the biographies of 400 persons living in the twentieth century who could be termed eminent and gifted. They concluded that, typically, most of the children who grew into eminence were introverted loners who followed their special interests almost to the exclusion of normal peer relationships.

These reports present us with a paradox. When one looks at gifted children, they seem well-adjusted and normal. When one looks at the way a gifted adult describes his childhood, he appears to have been lonely, isolated, shy and maladjusted. How can this paradox be explained?

A possible answer may, perhaps, be found in the kinds of instruments used for gathering the data. Terman used questionnaires and other objective devices which called for self-reports or for reports by others about the behaviour of the gifted. Most other researchers following Terman used sociometric questionnaires which found gifted children in general more popular than the average ones. For instance, in a study entitled "Is the Gifted Child a Socially Isolate?" Grace and Booth found that the sociometric status of gifted children in Grades 1 to 6 is a conclusive proof that they are not isolates.[15] When we look closely at sociometric data, we have to understand the instrument by which the data is measured. A sociometric test is a paper-and-pencil instrument which calls for one child to express a preference for another child or children.

We have often observed gifted children with good sociometric status (i.e. receiving many choices from their peers) spending their school recess time alone, reading in isolation from other children. In such an instance, an investigator using sociometric techniques would find the child to be involved and accepted in social relationships, while the investigator using observational methods would arrive at quite different conclusions. Sometimes the rejection of the gifted child by his peers, because of his special ways of thinking and dealing with a situation, can be discovered only by direct and systematic observation. Because of the biased nature of the instruments used to study social relations in the primary school, the social isolation of the gifted is not truly understood. Even if we accept data from sociometric tests, we should consider as well the reasons for children's choices.

If we knew something about the culture of children we can see how it is influenced by adult values. For example, popularity in primary school may be conferred on a child by virtue of a teacher's attitude, as when a teacher labels Johnny a bright child, or as popular, and

Johnny's peers take their cue accordingly. There are some research data which support this interpretation.[16] Children asked by the researchers to express their preference for other children did so, and the expressed preferences were compared with those of the teachers. In the third grade the correlation between teacher and student preference was .72; in the seventh grade the correlation dropped to .30; and finally, by grade eleven, the correlation fell to .10, which is statistically insignificant. As students grow older, they are apparently less and less influenced by teacher preference.

When children in primary schools were asked to nominate their gifted classmates, they selected the same children whom their teachers nominated.[17] When one remembers that teacher nominations miss between 20 and 40 percent of the gifted, one wonders about the misleading importance of the teachers' influence on children when it comes to determining the gifted child.

While high grades which reflect academic achievement, influence primary school teachers and pupils in the nomination and sociometric status of the gifted, the situation is rather different in high school, where the classic study of Coleman showed that academic brilliance is not valued highly by peers.[18] Other factors, such as athletic prowess for boys and attractiveness for girls were considered more important by the youth culture at that stage.

The gifted adolescent student who realizes this is faced with a choice. He can adopt the same perceptions and interests as his peers and, probably, abandon his intellectual interests and scholarly achievement, or he may ignore his peers' preference and continue as he is. In either case he is inviting trouble and introducing conflict and tension into his life. In our research on gifted underachievers, where we used sociometric tests in each class, the following results appeared. Although there were no significant differences in the number of sociometric choices which gifted achievers and underachievers received from their peers in the school, there were significant differences in the number of rejections they received. While the average number of rejections received by gifted achievers was 3.1, the average rejection of underachievers was only 1.6 (significant at $p < .005$). It seems that for some gifted children, underachievement might be a defence against rejection by their peers.

There is an additional explanation for this phenomenon which stands quite apart from the one which concerns itself with the nature of the data-gathering instruments. If it is assumed, as some evidence suggests, that there often is a deterioration in the social relationships of gifted children as they grow older, it may well be that the gifted adult reports are indeed accurate. As the gifted child passed from childhood to adolescence, he may have begun to feel, and indeed have been, more estranged, more lonely, and more isolated. In this case, the conclusion must be a straightforward admission that there is something inherent in the very nature of being intellectually gifted which disposes the adolescent to experience varying degrees of social maladjustment. What is this "something?"

First, there is the element of time. The gifted child does not have enough time allocated to social interactions where one learns social skills. Typically, either he or his parents have decided that he will enjoy a variety of "enrichment" activities, prominently including piano lessons, ballet classes, a foreign language, travel, museum trips, and sundry other learning opportunities. The problem begins for the gifted child, when, with a mounting load of activities, he simply does not have time to associate with his peers. We have found that the gifted child devotes eight-and-a-half hours per week to extra-curricular activities compared to the average child's three hours per week.

The gifted do develop their intellectual skills, but what of their social skills? It is not from books that one learns to interact; the emotions of successful friendships cannot be developed by intellectualization alone. The hazards, difficulties, and pleasures of interrelationships are all things that books cannot teach. Since one learns social skills mainly by interacting with others, it follows that the less room there is for interaction with others, the less opportunity there will be for the development of social skills.

Research has provided evidence of another aspect of social relationships: the importance of intelligence as an intervening variable in cementing friendships. O'Shea suggests that mutual friendships are more likely to follow mental than chronological age. That is, children of approximately the same range of intelligence tend to gravitate towards each other.[19] However, at the superior range in the distribution of intelligence, there are statistically fewer children of equal intelligence with whom the bright child can interact. He is unlikely to find in his classroom many other youngsters with similar abilities and interests with whom he can form friendships. As a consequence, the gifted child is likely to turn either to books or adults. Now, if the gifted child turns to books, electronics, stamp collecting, or insect mounting, he reinforces his isolation and his removal from his peers. Similarly if he turns to adults, he again separates himself from relationships with children. In either case he diminishes his chances of learning the rules of interaction.

In short, a variety of reasons cause the gifted adolescent's social adjustment to suffer as he grows older. These reasons may well account for the things the lonely scientist remembers when he is asked to recall his childhood. We can say that as a group the gifted are better adjusted than average students, but it is important to remain aware that intellectual giftedness can engender special problems in the social relationships.

The problems of underachievement and social relations which we have dealt with in this chapter are by no means all the problems which a gifted child can encounter because of his giftedness. However sensitivity to these problems, which appear most often in school, can assist a counsellor to plan preventive measures. It is his responsibility to introduce conditions which will reduce the danger of development of these problems and to provide timely intervention when he discerns signs of their presence.

6   Identification of the Gifted

The careful reader will have formed by now, with some degree of clarity and understanding, his own picture of the gifted. In this chapter we shall try to shed some light on the identification process. But first, let us ask ourselves, "Is there any need for the identification of the gifted?" Some people feel that gifted children, because of their special abilities, will be able to develop and achieve their highest potential without being identified as gifted and receiving special attention as a result. From what we have said until now, it should be clear that this is not so. What about the danger of discouragement because of lack of challenge? What about the threat that a developing pattern of underachievement will close the doors to higher education? What about social problems which may contribute to the disenchantment of the gifted and the consequent inability to develop their full intellectual capabilities.

As we have seen, gifted children have special intellectual needs, and an education system worth its name should provide, or at least attempt to provide, for them. Provision for the intellectual, and not only intellectual, needs of the gifted can take many forms, including specially designed programs which we shall present in the next chapter. The first steps however, should be to identify the gifted children who need these special programs, a task which is not as easy as it may appear. Even people such as teachers who are accustomed to working with children do not always know what to look for in a class of gifted children. We had an opportunity of visiting a special class for the gifted with a group of student teachers who tended to react with comment like, "*These* are gifted children?" and "What is so special about them?" We were not surprised at these comments, because most gifted children are first and foremost just children, behaving as do most children their age. There is no special halo of intellectual talent shining about their little heads to aid in the identification process.

Identification is needed in order to detect the particular aspects of intellectual giftedness; it should, however, be only the first step in a special program of assistance. If there is no intention of creating such a program, identification is useless. Putting an additional label on children not only does not help them, but may also cause more harm than one would expect. Identification which is not followed by positive action may even be the first step in the creation of a little monster. What would you think is likely to be the reaction to a child who goes around bragging: "My I.Q. is 152; what's yours?" The point is that identification *and* constructive assistance are basic contributors to the full utilization of the intellectual potential of these children.

When should identification start? Early! Already in kindergarten there are ways of identifying gifted children, but intelligence tests are not the measure to use. At this age intelligence tests are not reliable gauges; instead it is the child's behaviour which serves as the main clue to the presence of giftedness. Problem-solving with blocks, story-telling, drawing, and the Goodenough Draw-a-Person Tests are all helpful in the identification of gifted children at this early stage. Early identification of gifted children can help parents to understand and adopt healthy attitudes towards their special child; and to deal with such situations as: "My child is five and reads all day long, instead of playing with other children. Do I let him read, or do I stop him?" and "If I let him read now, will he be bored in the first grade?" Moreover, the identification permits the working out of policies and programs for the first years of schooling, such as whether a child should spend an entire year in the first grade, or whether his education should be accelerated. It also makes it possible to organize the children identified as gifted at the kindergarten level into special groups from the very beginning of their schooling. Teachers can be informed about the special abilities of the selected children and can be helped to deal with them.

Despite these advantages of early identification, one must beware of the seeming simplicity of identification at this early stage, because it lacks validity. It is the primary school years which form the stage for more valid, reliable, and complete identification. But what, exactly, should be identified? To put it in the simplest way: we endeavour to identify high levels of intelligence and other factors which research shows contribute to outstanding intellectual achievement. Such factors are: original thinking, creativity, curiosity drive, and many others with which we shall deal later on. The difficult task we take upon ourselves is to find the children with high intellectual potential and, from the start, to encourage and help them to fulfill that potential. Unfortunately, we are far from being able to delineate a failproof system by which to go. What can we do, and where do we start?

Our first step must be to define clearly what we are looking for. But, already, we need to apply caution, for there are two ways to go about it. On the one hand, we can define the intellectually gifted (as we have done in Chapter 2) as one who has an i.q. of 130 or more, and go from there. On the other hand, we can take into consideration and add to our definition factors of creativity like those that Torrance describes in his article "Broadening Concepts of Giftedness in the '70's." Our feeling is, however, that adding creativity and other special talents in a variety of fields clouds our picture instead of clarifying it. Granted, one may be very creative without having a high I.Q. No one has ever pondered over the question as to whether or not Gauguin had a high I.Q. We are fully aware that intellectual giftedness, as defined and measured primarily by I.Q., will undoubtedly leave out some of those creative individuals who are gifted in fields such as, for instance, the arts. In this book as we have already pointed out, we are, by design, focussing exclusively on the individuals whose giftedness is based on high intelligence. Our first step in identification, therefore, will be to find the restricted group of children (the upper 3 per cent of the population) who all share one characteristic, an I.Q. of 130 or above.

There will, of course, be many differences among these children, not only in creativity, but also in emotional development and many other measurable characteristics. When one deals with a restricted range in one particular variable, there always exist a sizable variability in aspects which are not directly a function of the particular variable in question. Therefore, we will look for high intelligence, but also try to take into consideration all other important variables theoretically linked to it.

Our final question is: "How do we identify?" In reply, we shall outline a program of identification which involves work, time, good planning, and the capacity of pulling together the relevant materials. It uses as "identifiers" the counsellors, teachers, parents, and peers of the children. We would like to draw attention to the fact that measuring devices have their drawbacks. This is why we stress in our program a variety of evidence from many sources. Since we are dealing with such complex concepts as human giftedness, the more evidence we have, the better our prediction will be.

The Identification Program

The program which we present makes use of both the objective and the subjective approaches. The objective approach uses standardized measures and arrives at scores on which children can be compared. The subjective approach uses observations made by those who know the child well and interact with him in a variety of situations. The observations we shall use in our program are made by teachers, parents, and peers. The counsellor's task will be to centralize, integrate, and evaluate the gathered information.

1 OBJECTIVE APPROACH

The objective approach is based mainly on intelligence testing which, we hope, is intelligent. For those who are familiar with the intricacies of measurement, it is clear that to adhere to a rigid cut-off point is nonsense. The difference between an I.Q. of 128 and an I.Q. of 130 is insignificant; certainly a child with an I.Q. of 128 should not be excluded from a program for gifted children if the other capacities for which we are looking are present. In addition to intelligence testing, school grades form another objective measure which should be taken into consideration. There is no doubt that school grades are somewhat less objective than test scores, but since they reflect many aspects of the child's effort in the classroom situation, they should be considered. Finally, achievement tests, in which children are compared with national norms of academic achievement, can also be helpful in the objective approach.

The use of intelligence tests is a two-step approach. The first step is group intelligence testing. The second is individual testing of those children whom group tests have identified as having high potential. Lately, I.Q. tests have been severely criticized, but to paraphrase Churchill's remark about democracy, we feel that intelligence tests are the worst possible instruments for identifying giftedness, excepting all others!

So we start the identification process by a screening procedure, using group tests of intelligence. The great advantage of the group test is that it is a very rapid procedure which saves time and money and gives quite a good picture of the abilities of the children who are tested. But group tests have a few important drawbacks. First, since the ceiling of group intelligence tests is rather low, the tests' power of discrimination of high levels of intelligence is also rather low. Many gifted children finish the test, and could have done more, before the end of the allotted time; consequently, the high abilities of some gifted children are not discovered. Secondly, the correlations between the group and the individual tests, especially for the higher levels of intelligence, are not too high. Some children who receive an I.Q. score of 120 on a group test may achieve that of 140 on individual testing. This means, that, when using the group tests for screening purposes, we have to lower our criteria. If we want to identify, let us say, children with an I.Q. of 130 or higher for special programs, we need to lower the cut-off point in the group tests to about 120. This cut-off point will separate from the general population about 15 per cent who have a high potential.

Additional inconveniences inherent in group testing are its tendency to penalize those who have reading problems and who come from a different culture. There is no way of helping the child who cannot follow the instructions because he cannot read them (reading problems), or cannot comprehend the way they are worded (cultural differences). This leads us to one of the basic difficulties of group testing, the fact that it does not allow us to get at the child himself. The tests are given to him in his normal classroom situation. Very often he does not understand the significance of these questions; they look like a standard routine examination in, say, English or History. What if the child is gifted but lacks interest, because he incorporates the whole experience as part and parcel of all the other boring examinations? What if as a result, he lacks the motivation to work on the test to the best of his ability? What if he starts doodling with his pencil and never gets to the questions? We have no way *ex post facto* to return to the child and distinguish his giftedness from his lack of motivation. These are serious problems which may mean overlooking just that child we are seeking.

How can we counterbalance the drawbacks of the first step? One way is to look at school grades. Parallel with group testing, the counsellor should collect the pupil's grades and compare them with the child's scores on the group test. The counsellor will find that the majority of children with high I.Q.'s will have high grades. Examining the grades and the test scores he can ask himself, "What is the difference between straight A's from a child with an I.Q. of 115 and straight A's from a child with an I.Q. of 150?" The next step, individual testing, will then include those children with high scores in group testing as well as those children with low scores but consistently high grades. Children with average grades but with high scores on these tests are also worthy of attention. Individual testing will permit us to distinguish those among them who are gifted.

The advantages of individual tests are manifold, but their main drawback is that they are time-consuming. This is probably the principal reason why so few school systems use individual tests as well as group measurements in their identification programs. Individual tests, however, permit us to learn quite a lot about the child. Not only does one see how the child actually works, how he deals with difficulties, and what his stronger and weaker points are, but one can learn quite a lot from the differences between the sub-scores, about the child's intellectual functions and his emotional, social, and motorial problems. The clinical uses of the Wechsler Intelligence Scales for Children (WISC) are very well known. The Terman-Binet test also gives a wealth of information. In 1969, Meeker presented in her book a way of inferring from the Binet test about 50 factors from the Guilford structure of the intellect model.[1]

One last word about individual intelligence tests: we believe that too much energy is wasted on the intelligence versus creativity controversy. It would be very helpful if psychologists would try instead to integrate a scale which measures originality into the known intelligence tests. Such integrated tests would furnish results which would show both the convergent and the divergent aspects in the subject's intellectual approach. Some pioneer work along these lines was started by Bruch who proposed a re-weighting of the Binet scores which would give a "creative age."[2] This "creative age" could then be compared with the mental age of the child and some tentative deductions could be made concerning the relationship between the convergent and the divergent abilities of the child.

2 SUBJECTIVE APPROACH

Up to now, we have looked at the objective approaches for identifying the gifted and, by doing so in a school setting, we will probably have singled out the majority of gifted children. However, there may be some children who demonstrate intellectual giftedness in ways other than scholastic achievement or group I.Q. scores. The qualities of these children cannot pass unnoticed by those who come in contact with them be they teachers, parents, or classmates. These people become "subjective identifiers" whose difficult task it is to tap these very qualities, using subjective approaches. Children identified by this method should also be included in the individual testing program.

The Teacher as Identifier

If teachers could nominate the gifted children in their classroom, this would be the fastest, cheapest, and most convenient way of identifying gifted children. Many researchers since Terman's time, have tried to evaluate the efficacy of teacher nomination. Practically all of them have demonstrated that teachers miss from 40 to 60 per cent of the gifted pupil in their classes.[3] Why are teachers not good identifiers of the gifted? We can start to understand some of the difficulties teachers face in nominating the gifted by looking at the first attempt to secure teachers' nominations made by Terman in the 1920's. Teachers were asked to supply the names of one to three pupils whom they regarded as the most intelligent in their classes. They were instructed not just to base their judgement on school marks, but also on such qualities as originality, reasoning ability, common sense, and the extent and accuracy of information, curiosity, vocabulary, and independence of judgement.[4]

One cannot but wonder how the teachers utilized these instructions. What is "originality?" What is "common sense?" And what is "extent and accuracy of information?" Even with operational definitions of these concepts it would be very difficult to assume that all teachers would use the same criteria for selection. It is probably logical to assume that teachers would often select as the most intelligent pupils those children with the highest marks, on the grounds that they had given the best marks to the most capable pupil. It would be hard to argue this point with them because the bright student is the teacher's living proof, if not the only one, that he is succeeding in his job. Good pupils who learn well and do their assignments faithfully symbolize for the teacher his success in his role. His job is to teach, to transmit information which is then to be understood and assimilated by the student. To do this, he has (he hopes) the right tools and the right experience. It is not only a matter of a particular experience, but also one of a special outlook. The teacher's whole outlook on the pupil is based primarily on what he knows his own job to be, how he intends to perform it, and what his standards are for classroom behaviour. His outlook, then, is totally a function of his role as a teacher and his view of the child's role as a pupil.

Role identification influences the way teachers, as well as other professionals, perceive others and how they see others perceiving them. In research which studied children's behaviour problems as viewed by teachers and psychologists, it was shown that teachers perceived children's behavioural problems, such as disobedience, impertinence, tattling, and over-criticism, as more severe than did psychologists.[5] On the other hand, psychologists saw as more severe, dishonesty, depression, shyness, dependency, and daydreaming. Two related phenomena work together in creating the special outlook which dominates a profession: the particular professional framework and the ensuing role of identification. These phenomena are also at the basis of the different ways in which teachers and psychologists identify the gifted. Nothing in a teacher's experience prepares him for the difficult task of identifying the exceptional student with a very high I.Q. These students are not run of the mill; they are rare birds, and you only find three of these among one hundred.

Up to now, we have seen that psychologists are dissatisfied with teachers' nominations. But one can look at the problem differently. Teachers have been asked to identify pupils with the highest I.Q.'s, but suppose that the teacher should say to a psychologist: "Please identify the most outstanding pupil in history, geography, and literature." In this case, it is the teacher who has the appropriate identification tools and the psychologist who will be at a loss. We can easily predict the ensuing paper entitled "How Psychologists miss 50 per cent of the Best Historians and Writers."

We believe that psychologists should not ask teachers to guess what they, the psychologists, can certainly measure more accurately. They should seek the teacher's help in identifying those aspects of giftedness which cannot be tapped with tests. Ideally, the counsellor or the school psychologist, during his in-service training with teachers, should organize discussion groups in which he can detail the intellectual behavioural characteristics of the gifted on which teachers can then base their judgement. We are presenting a checklist for teachers which includes the characteristics which they should be looking for. We have taken special care to provide the teacher with easy-to-use guidelines. Many such lists have been proposed in Canada[6] and the United States.[7]

We believe that a checklist which is to be a useful working tool for teachers should have the following characteristics:

1 *Brevity.* If the list includes too many items, it may discourage teachers. Let us face it, it is very difficult to work with a lengthy list for each child when you have 40 pupils.

2 *Clarity of definitions.* Vague formulas like "open mindedness" leave a lot to guesswork (which is precisely what should be avoided). Of course definitions are still open to a variety of interpretations, but they are helpful for a better understanding. Giving teachers the same definition will allow more reliable comparisons of teachers' ratings.

3 *Teacher-oriented.* There is no sense in asking a teacher to evaluate anything but what he can readily observe in the school situation. Therefore, variable aspects such as richness of vocabulary and memory, which are tapped better by intelligence tests than by subjective evaluation, should be excluded.

The proposed checklist has three parts. The first part consists of ten characteristics, which are defined and which the teacher is asked to evaluate.

1 *Capacity for integration.* Perceives relations between seemingly unrelated areas of knowledge; presents ideas as a result of integration.

2 *Critical thinking.* Finds missing links and incongruities; expresses constructive criticism and non-conforming ideas.

3 *Curiosity.* Asks questions about cause and effect; investigates additional aspects of things learned.

4 *Facility of expression.* Is able to present his ideas clearly and richly; expresses complex ideas in simple and understandable ways.

5 *Love of reading.* Is interested in all written material, be it literature, science, journals, or encyclopaedias.

6 *Need for achievement.* Works according to own standard of excellence; invests his best efforts in any task.

7 *Originality.* Generates new and rare views; finds unusual but better solutions to problems; proposes novel points of view.

8 *Perseverance.* Is not discouraged by temporary failure; concentrates on task in spite of attractive outside stimuli and keeps at it till finished.

9 *Quickness of comprehension.* Responds quickly and adequately to new stimuli; learns rapidly; progresses faster than most.

10 *Special interest.* Shows high involvement in one or more areas of interest (science or arts); vigorously investigates many aspects of his chosen area in depth.

The second part gives the teacher a way of evaluating each characteristic. A simple rating scale with the following four points could be helpful:

1 Never	3 Often
2 Rarely	4 As a rule

The third part consists of a chart, "Teachers' Identification Guide For Gifted Students," with space for the names of the pupils in the teacher's class and a column for each of the characteristics of the list (see Figure 5). The teacher will have this guide on one page and on a separate page the one-page list of the ten characteristics and their definitions. After filling in the names of the pupils in his class, the teacher will look at the first child's name, think about the first characteristic (capacity for integration), and, after thinking about the child and the characteristic, he will decide what score to give him. The teacher then proceeds to the next characteristic, decides on the score, and so on until the child has been scored for all ten characteristics. He does the same for all the pupils in the class. The total score should serve as a rough guideline for comparing the children. Those with high scores should be included in the individual intelligence-test program, and those presenting irregularities in their scores should become a question of judgement for the counsellor.

Such an identification guide has many uses. First, it will help in the process of identification by bringing in new elements which otherwise would remain undiscovered. Second, it will increase the teacher's awareness of some aspects of children's behaviour which are not generally in the focus of his attention. Third, as the teacher is helped to observe systematically the forms of behaviour relevant to the characteristics of giftedness, the guide may be the basis for his deeper understanding of the term. For example a teacher may observe how many times a week Alice takes out new books from the library. Finally,

Fig. 5 TEACHER'S IDENTIFICATION GUIDE FOR GIFTED STUDENTS

Teacher's Name .... Grade .... Date....................

	CAPACITY FOR INTE-GRATION	CRITICAL THINKING	CURI-OSITY	FACILITY OF EX-PRESSION	LOVE OF READING	NEED FOR ACHIEVE-MENT	ORIGI-NALITY	PERSE-VERANCE	QUICKNESS OF COM-PREHENSION	SPECIAL INTERESTS	TOTAL
Ted	3	4	4	3	3	4	4	2	3	4	34
Alice	2	1	3	2	3	3	3	3	3	3	26
Bob	1	2	2	1	1	1	2	1	1	2	14
Carol	4	3	4	4	3	4	3	3	2	4	34

comparisons of ratings from teachers who teach different disciplines to the same class may be very valuable in gaining understanding of the reasons why a child may be very high in, say, curiosity and originality in one subject and very low in those qualities in others.

Since a child spends half of his waking life in school, the teacher is one of the best judges of his behaviour and personality as shown in the classroom situation.

Parents as Identifiers

What does the child do when he is at home? How does he relate to his family, his neighbours, and his friends? Does he spend all afternoon playing football with the gang and need almost to be forced to sit down for ten minutes to look reluctantly into his school assignments, or does he spend the afternoon browsing avidly in Daddy's library? Is he at a loss for something to do, nagging Mummy to help him fill his time, or is he immersed in building an airplane following his own design?

No one can observe a child's behaviour at home better than his parents, especially his mother. She can best look back and describe how the helpless, dependent, crying infant became the bright, independent, assertive child. Even though a mother does not use systematic ways of comparison, other children are always around. The young mother seeks the society of other mothers in order to conduct "brag groups" which are in reality comparative studies in child development. As long as the stories of "what my child does" are similar to other stories, there is a yardstick of normal development. But when the tale of what our child does is very different from the other stories, questions begin to arise. A mother may wonder what her child does that others do not. All studies of the gifted describe precociousness as one of the main development traits. The gifted child does everything earlier than other children; he walks, talks, and reads early. He asks questions about the origins of the world earlier than one would expect. He remembers what he is told and builds his next question on that; he has many more interests than children his age and develops them with amazing skill.

No teacher, no I.Q. test, no creativity test will be able to tell us the developmental story of the precocious child. His teacher may single him out, and I.Q. tests will reveal his superior score, but only his parents can describe his involvement with hobby interests, his enthusiasm for his favourite projects, and his persistence at executing his inventions. The parent, therefore, is not only a helpful but an indispensable partner in the identification process.

But can a parent give a objective description of his child? Thank heavens, parents are not objective. And identification is a hard task for parents, not only because of their blessed subjectivity, but also because of the lack of a framework for comparison. Contrary to the classroom where most of the situations are standardized and where it is easy to see how a majority of children behave and react at a given age, the family as a framework consists of much more complex dynamics. In the home, the parents' expectations for a child may vary daily and may be dependent on moods, sibling behaviour, mother's preoccupations, or the child's own exigencies. On the other hand, every child in a classroom is well aware of expectations which his teacher clearly specifies. A child must return assignments on a certain day, without any considerations for father's mood, mother's preoccupations, or his own whims. Therefore, while a teacher is immediately aware of a child who does not behave like all (or most) of the others, parents do not have such a clear picture of a child's discrepancies. In other words, a teacher constantly has handy criteria for comparison; the parents do not. Nevertheless, research has shown that parents are as good "identifiers" as teachers are at the kindergarten level[8] and in the primary school year.[9]

This being so, the need for a structured checklist for parents becomes evident. To be useful, such a list needs to meet the following specifications:

1 *Brevity.* A checklist which is too long may "frighten" the parents. People have a tendency – well known by psychologists – not to answer long questionnaires.

2 *Clarity of definition.* This is for the same reasons we mentioned for the teacher's checklist.

3 *Exclusively home- and neighbourhood oriented.* It should include those characteristics which may be observed from the child's longitudinal past history as well as those characteristics which define his present behaviour in the home situation. Aspects tapped by the teacher in the classroom should be excluded.

A good checklist for parents should focus mainly on the following aspects: developmental history, parent-child relations, special interests and hobbies, daily schedule, and friendships.

Developmental history should include things like age of walking and talking, when the child started to show interest in reading, in numbers, in making up stories, and his health and physical history.

In the area of parent-child relationship, the range of the possible quality of interactions is practically unlimited. However, in a checklist one needs to focus on some main points such as:

How does the child react to parental demands?

Is he overly dependent or does he strongly assert his autonomy?

Is he usually compliant or has he turned into the tyrant of the household?

As far as interests are concerned, both parents and counsellors know that the average child passes through periods of interest in various and sundry things from stories to insects, and passing through stamps and bottle caps. What is common to these interests is that they come and go, creating, while they last, superlative excitement. However, one may find children who become interested in a specific activity, such as the collection of stones, and who will advance from the run-of-the-mill pebble found in the open field to stones of all kinds, to mineral rocks, all the while becoming more and more enthusiastic about their hobby, looking up in encyclopaedias, and visiting libraries in search of a further information. A hobby like this absorbs a great deal of the child's daily routine. Indeed, the daily activities of a child form another important element of scheduling which stands out. The fact that the child understands very early in his life that time has limits and, therefore, allows rational time spaces for specific activities; and, on the other hand, the fact that there seems to be no limit to his activities, make for a schedule which is self-imposed and tight.

As a matter of fact, this very fullness of his daily life is one of the important characteristics differentiating the gifted from the average child. Does all this hectic activity allow the gifted child to develop socially? Answers to this question certainly need to be part of a parent checklist or questionnaire. Is the child gregarious? Does he make friends easily? Does he need the company of buddies? Is he a loner, rather shy, aloof? Who are his friends? Are they his age or are they older? And how much older? If and when he brings them home, what do they do? Do they play Cowboys and Indians, watch t.v., or work on projects and inventions?

It would be difficult, probably impossible, to point to any generalized pattern in the socialization of gifted children. However, precious insight can be gained from a careful description of all the observations made by parents. Many good checklists or questionnaires exist for parents in professional literature.[10,11]

In what form should the parents' identification guide be presented? Both the checklist and the open questionnaire have their advantages and inconveniences. A checklist is easy to fill in, does not necessitate much time, can be rapidly scored, and have a comparative value. But, because a checklist is too restricted, parents cannot always express valuable points freely. On the other hand, in an open questionnaire, the advantages of the checklist become disadvantages and the inconveniences become strong points. Parents can freely describe on the questionnaire all kinds of behaviour without being restricted to the items of the checklist. Therefore, the counsellor who wishes to use parents as "identifiers" should weigh the pros and cons of each system and decide which is more advantageous in the particular situation.

Which parents should be included in the process of identification? Ideally the answer to that question is to include all parents, because sometimes we are in for some surprises. The child who is quiet, shy, and unobtrusive in the classroom may have an exciting, full, and interesting span of activities outside the school. How can one learn about the richness of this child's life, except by receiving the information from his parents? Still, one should be aware that ideal situations are rarely obtained in real life. Since it is well known in research that one can never reach a whole population with questionnaires, particularly in a case where the motivation for the average parent to reply might be very low, it would be more economic in effort and in time to ask for help in the process of identification of the gifted from those parents who have children with a promising i.q (as it was found in the group i.q. test) or those children nominated by their teachers.

To conclude our remarks on the parental contribution to the process of identification, we should like to add that parents' checklists or questionnaires not only aid the identification process but also serve as sources of valuable and important information on children's behaviour and development at home, especially when teachers and counsellors are working with them in special programs.

Children as Identifiers

Children behave differently when they are with other children than when they are with adults. Adult-dominated situations are more restrictive to the child than children-dominated situations are. The mere presence of an adult among children will subtly change the general pattern of their behaviour. The peer group also has some restrictive influences caused by its own inner dynamics and its inherent rules and laws, which have an impact on all its members. Thus, the presence of the teacher and the restrictive quality of the classroom situation may cause the child to exhibit certain facets of his personality; the dynamics of the peer group will encourage expression of other facets. Children and adults differ in their judgements of others mainly because these very judgements are a function of differing points of view, values, outlooks, and priorities on the part of both children and adults. Therefore, a more complete picture of a child's personality can be obtained

Counselling the Intellectually Gifted Child

by integrating the judgements of the peer group with those of other identifiers. Research has shown that peers are as good as teachers in the process of identifying the gifted.[12] This does not mean that peers nominate the same children as teachers do. What it does mean is that the percentage of the gifted indicated by the nomination of the peer group is more or less equal to that of the teachers.

What is the best way of using peer-group nomination? We consider the most useful approach to be the "Guess Who" technique, employing a simple and straightforward list of questions, which taps a child's judgements of his peers. This technique consists of the creation of fictitious characters who exhibit the qualities one wants to have the children evaluate. For example, "There is a child in this classroom who often invents new and interesting games; guess who? . . . ." If most of the answers to this question nominate a particular child, it is very probable that a trait of creativity and originality has been located which might not have been discovered by other measures. An added advantage of the "Guess Who" technique is that children like it, and they are interested in the task which is very different from their usual ones. Additionally, it can be scored rapidly and easily.

What types of questions should one include in the identification process with peers? We reiterate that it is very important for the counsellor who makes up the questions for this test to remember to orient them exclusively to the peer group. Here are a few examples of aspects one might want to use in making up a questionnaire. Guess who:

Makes decisions followed by most other children.
Influences other children to work towards a goal.
Is often consulted by other children.
Invents new and interesting activities.
Is appealed to as a judge in conflicts.
Helps others in schoolwork and assignments.

After he has accumulated data from objective and subjective sources in the various stages of the identification process, the counsellor is left with a small percentage of children. To this group he then administers the individual I.Q. tests.

Of course, we do not exclude the possibility of adding any additional type of test to the identification program. Those who value the creativity test highly or who want to learn other things which might be important in their particular view of giftedness, should use any tests they wish. These might be tests for creativity, anxiety, locus of control, art appreciation, or leadership, among others. We wish to stress again, however, that we are looking for the intellectually gifted. We are positive that most children in this category can be discovered by using the devices described in this chapter. After we have administered the individual intelligence tests, some 3 to 5 per cent of the school population will remain. This minority is the population we are after; most of the children will have an I.Q. of 130 and above; others will have a somewhat lower I.Q. but will possess the promising capacities which were discovered by the additional identification measures.

We know from research that people with high, but not the highest, intelligence and the greatest degree of persistence are likely to achieve more than those people who combine the highest intelligence with less persistence.[13] Cox, the author of this research, reached this conclusion after an intensive study of 300 biographies of outstanding contributors to humanity's progress. Others have reached similar conclusions after having studied the lives of eminent scientists[14] and writers.[15]

If this is so, one wonders why we do not investigate persistence, perseverance, and drive for work. While some paper-and-pencil tests measuring perseverance are available, they are rather crude. What is needed is a meaningful and, if possible, behavioural way of predicting perseverance. We have devised such a measure and would like to propose it for counsellors interested in discovering those gifted children who will possibly use their high intellectual capacities and contribute significantly to science in the future.

Our approach consists of proposing to the gifted children that they write a paper on any subject of their choosing. The best work will be published in, perhaps, a university journal, and will be rewarded with a special prize. The children are told that they have a month to work on their project and that all the books they need and many others related to their field of interest, are available in a special room in the library. They are informed that they can consult the books only on the premises; the books cannot be taken out. In this case, the librarian is the main agent of observation. He or she will keep a record of the comings and goings of the children, the time they spend reading and studying, and the number of books they use. The librarian's observations are probably one of the best measures of intellectual perseverance one can find. The results of the children's efforts, in terms of the quality of their projects as they are judged by experts in the various fields, will be another important measure of the intellectual effort.

We started such a project in May, 1974, and the results were striking in terms of the huge differences in behaviour between highly intelligent children with the same I.Q. and the same age level We definitely distinguished two groups: those who fully utilized the facilities of the library for many hours and those who played games around the library. The predictive value of this behavioural test is still a question mark,

Counselling the Intellectually Gifted Child

Fig. 6   THE IDENTIFICATION PROCESS

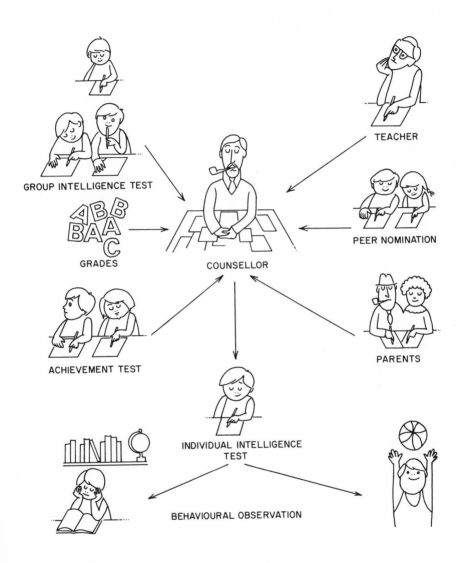

GROUP INTELLIGENCE TEST

TEACHER

GRADES

COUNSELLOR

PEER NOMINATION

ACHIEVEMENT TEST

PARENTS

INDIVIDUAL INTELLIGENCE
TEST

BEHAVIOURAL OBSERVATION

and only a long-term follow-up will reveal whether the qualities of drive or perseverance in the gifted young who are interested in science will produce the eminent scientists of the future. In any case we consider this avenue of investigation to be of sufficient merit to be included in a chapter on identification.

Figure 6 (page 73) presents a graphic illustration of the main points in the process of identification.

7   Special Programs for the Gifted

The mere mention of special programs for the gifted is, for some educators and the public at large, like waving a red rag before a bull. For such people the very idea is undemocratic and viewed as elitist and unjust. As we saw in the first chapter, the idea of special schools and special programs for the underprivileged and for the intellectually retarded is well accepted by all. Why then do people react emotionally to the idea of special help for the gifted? Among the many possible reaons we see three as the most important:

Some people worry about equality in education. Equality in education is wrongly perceived as uniformity in education. "The same educational program for all children of the same age level" is the principle at the basis of legislation in education.

Second, some people feel that the intellectually gifted do not need any special help, believing that if they are gifted, they will advance anyhow according to their high abilities.

Third, some people fear that high mental ability is strongly related to some kind of mental maladjustment. In other words, one really should not encourage the development of high mental capacities because "genius and madness are akin."

We believe that all these objections are unwarranted. First of all, equality in education should not mean uniformity but rather a giving to all children equal opportunity for the best utilization of their individual potential. Although many gifted children do realize their high intellectual capacities, this is far from being true for all the gifted. And one should remember that the Terman study clearly showed that there is no significant relation between giftedness and mental maladjustment; the contrary is more often the case.

The special needs of the intellectually gifted students point to some insufficiences in the educational setting. If education took into consideration individual differences in abilities and could give each student the opportunity of advancing at his own pace, there would be no need for special programs for the gifted.

New approaches in education stress the need for flexibility in order to help each child to achieve full utilization of his capacities (or growth). The teaching machines of the 1950's and today's computer-aided instruction have as their main objective just that. Each child, working independently, would be able to progress more quickly or more slowly and to use more simple or more complex material, in short, to progress at his own pace.

Individualized teaching, one of the newest educational approaches, which comes from England, has a similar objective, that of making it possible for each child to direct his own learning. This approach stresses the importance of the teacher's recognition and encouragement of each child's individuality in order to help the child to develop a favourable view of himself and of his abilities.[1] We are sure that all teachers would agree with this point of view. Unfortunately, this is closer to the ideal than to the reality, so long as the educational establishment must face the enormous task of educating all children with all their existing differences in groups of thirty to forty.

In the educational setting as it exists today, the special needs of gifted children are not totally ignored; a few ways of dealing with them have been, and are being, tried out. Three main types of special programs for the gifted exist: acceleration, grouping, and enrichment. There are of course many subdivisions and variations to these approaches. In the United States, Getzels and Dillon enumerated twenty-seven different programs encompassing a variety of activities, all of which can be traced back to the three main approaches mentioned earlier.[2] New approaches should certainly be tried out. Gifted children can, and should, be helped in different ways. The more efficient we become in our ways of working with them, the more approaches we will use and the better our understanding of giftedness will become.

In devising new programs, however, we must be continually on the alert to the danger of giving new names to old things, like regarding "Saturday Seminars" as something different from enrichment. Furthermore, when a new program is developed and tried out, a systematic follow-up of the program and its effects is of paramount importance. Teachers, counsellors, psychologists, and all those interested in the field need concrete and detailed data such as a description of the program and of the steps involved in its preparation, implementation, and follow-up to help them in their work. The systematic description of all the steps in a program, whether it is successful or unsuccessful, helps in the advancement of dealing with the gifted.

In this chapter we shall attempt to describe the three main approaches to the education of the gifted. These programs are basically integrated in the school system. In addition, we shall present a rather different approach, which integrates not only the school, but also the parents and the community as a whole. It is important that the counsellor understand the characteristics of each of these programs, and the advantages and disadvantages, in order that he may use this knowledge for their implementation.

Acceleration

Acceleration can be described as changes made by the school which help students complete a given program in less time than is usually allotted. Such changes can be made at different stages in the education process, as, for example, early admission to the first grade, skipping a grade, or learning the curriculum of three years in two years' time.

When a child in the first grade reads perfectly well and is much more advanced than his class in mathematics, it seems natural to transfer him to the second grade. Children who demonstrate a capacity for quick learning and who possess a wealth of knowledge unusual for their age, usually demonstrate a faster pace with which they are able to step up the traditional ladder of the educational system. This system is constructed for the average child, and it prescribes six years of learning for the accumulation of the knowledge necessary to start junior high school. If the child arrives at this basic knowledge in less time, say, in four or five years, the acceleration process takes his personal rhythm into consideration and permits him to go through the "regular steps" at a quicker pace. This seems rather logical and maybe even obvious.

In 1965, Goldberg pointed out that although almost anyone could think of at least one person whose life had been ruined or made unhappy by acceleration, it was difficult to find any research study which documented any harmful effects of acceleration on a group of students.[3] In 1947, Terman and Oden had already recommended, as a result of their research, that children with I.Q.,s of 135 or more should be accelerated for college entrance at 17; a majority of these students would be better off if they could be prepared to enter college at 16.[4]

During the 1950's, acceleration became a popular research topic. Many projects investigated its results, and since practically all results showed a positive trend, interest in this area of research faded away. However, it is sad to note that in spite of these results, acceleration is as rare today as it was before the publication of the results of the investigations. Let us glance rapidly at some of the representative research projects on acceleration and their results.

Some authors were interested in the early entrance to first grade. In all school systems the entrance to school is a function of chronological age. In most countries this age is six; in certain school systems, however, younger children are admitted to first grade if they have a mental age at least a year ahead of their chronological age. How do these gifted but younger children adjust to school from the intellectual, social, and emotional points of view? In 1954, Monderer compared 138 gifted pupils who entered school at the age of five with 468 pupils (also gifted) who started at the age of six. He found that the younger children not only had better school achievement as reflected by grades, but also were better adjusted socially, as measured by socio-metric tests.[5] A recent investigation in Israel by Weisman compared 61 gifted children who entered school at the prescribed ages with 47 children who entered school one year earlier (the median i.q. for both groups was 135). When they reached the fifth grade the two groups of children were compared in terms of their school grades, their socio-metric status, and their manifest anxiety. No significant differences were found in school grades or anxiety between the two groups but the children who had been admitted to school earlier had better sociometric status.[6]

Let us now look into acceleration at the high school and college level. In 1956, Pressey studied the effect of acceleration on scientific achievement.[7] The diagram opposite (figure 7, page 79) shows the percentage of outstanding contributions of students who finished col-lege at different ages.

It is clear from this diagram that there is a direct relationship be-tween the age of finishing college studies and outstanding contribu-tions in the field of science. Lehman's classic study which we men-tioned in the first chapter shows how age influences achievement. In Terman's follow-up study of gifted children as adults, significantly more accelerated pupils were in group A (the successful adults) than in group C (the unsuccessful ones).

When he commended acceleration, Terman noted in his report that maladjustment did result in some individuals, but that, in general, the maladjustment was a temporary feeling of inferiority which was later overcome. Nevertheless, Terman believed that it was important that each child be regarded on an individual basis.[8]

His emphasis on the individual consideration of each child is espe-cially significant for counsellors. In spite of the fact that research evidence indicates that acceleration has no negative effects for *most* children, problems do arise for some of them. One should remember that research is based on statistical averages. Statistical averages are important in understanding general laws, but must be handled cau-tiously when one is dealing with individuals. There is a standard joke, well known among statisticians, which warns that one can drown in a river whose average depth is three feet.

Acceleration is most often positive, although in some cases it can be destructive. The famous case of William Sidis, the child prodigy, should be a red light for the too enthusiastic and automatic use of acceleration. William Sidis's story draws attention to various aspects

Counselling the Intellectually Gifted Child

Fig. 7 OUTSTANDING CONTRIBUTIONS RELATED TO COLLEGE
GRADUATION AGE

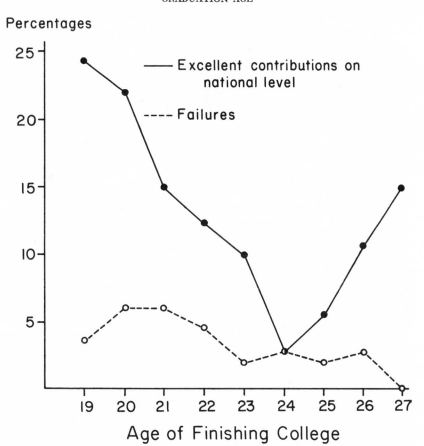

Percentages

— Excellent contributions on national level

---- Failures

Age of Finishing College

of special education for the gifted. William's father devised a home educational program for his son, to tap and develop rapidly and intensively most of the boy's unusual intellectual capability.

Barbe and Adler described William Sidis's educational history in a report published in 1972.[9] They noted that William could read at the age of two and that he used a typewriter, writing in English and French at the age of four. The boy entered Grade 1 and, within six months, passed through seven grades. By the time he was eight, William was sufficiently skilled in mathematics to devise a table of logarithms on a base of twelve instead of ten. At nine years of age, the boy passed the Harvard University entrance examinations, although he was not allowed to matriculate until he was eleven.

William seems to have been in good health, and the only negative reports on his physical development come from his Harvard days where he showed little motor ability. His social and emotional development are difficult to ascertain. Some claim that in his earlier years, there was no trace of maladjustment, but that, on the contrary, William took himself for granted and did not regard his precocity as anything out of the ordinary. In his early days at Harvard, however, he was described as "egotistical" and "one-sided" and at the age of seventeen he was characterized as an "intolerable pig." As an adult William destroyed in one swoop all the dreams of future achievement and contribution to society which were centred upon him. After his brilliant career at Harvard, he took great care to avoid any job which required thinking or decision-making. For twenty years he wandered aimlessly working as a heavy labourer.

In their study, Barbe and Adler posed pertinent questions about the unproductive life of William Sidis. Was William, in his aimless wanderings, in fact searching for a lost childhood, companionship, or autonomy, or was he only seeking the human world rather than the realm of ideas?[10]

After talking about averages and statistics as they relate to acceleration, we went to the other extreme by presenting an exceptional exception. The counsellor should draw the conclusion that acceleration in general is advisable and, if used wisely, it can promote the cognitive, social and emotional development of most of the gifted children.

However, before actually counselling acceleration for an individual child, the counsellor should consider a few important factors. First, the time factor is, it seems, an important one. Are there periods during which acceleration is more advisable than at others? Acceleration for a gifted first grader may mean the difference between a good start in life in which he feels challenged and stimulated, and one in which he develops attitudes of boredom and even of negativism towards school and study. The point is that a very appropriate time for acceleration is at the beginning of a child's school life. As he progresses up the scholastic ladder, he gradually forms his friendships and pal relationships and becomes part of a peer group. At that stage, acceleration could mean a cruel separation from a world of friends which at that point constitutes the child's main asset of models. Acceleration during this peer-group period can dangerously harm the child's social adjustment, since after his separation from his own group, it might be very difficult for him to enter the highly cohesive cliques of the next class.

Another very appropriate time for acceleration is at college entrance and during college, when age differences are not so clearly distinguishable. In special cases, it is, of course, up to the counsellor to judge

Counselling the Intellectually Gifted Child

whether acceleration may be advised at other times during a child's school life.

This leads to the other factors which are part of the counsellor's judgements concerning acceleration. It is clear, from research, that acceleration has been proven positive and advisable in most cases of giftedness. However, caution should be exercised, and we want to draw attention to the factors underlying this circumspection.

PHYSICAL DEVELOPMENT

Before advising acceleration, the counsellor should carefully examine the level of physical development of the child. If an important gap exists between his physical development and that of his classmates, this will certainly have some implication for his adjustment in a higher class. In such a case it might be wise to wait and follow the child's physical development and to decide about acceleration at a later date, when the gap has diminished.

EMOTIONAL MATURITY

In some gifted children there is a serious discrepancy between their intellectual and their emotional maturity. When a child's level of emotional maturity is below the norms of his age, acceleration should be avoided or at least postponed.

SOCIAL RELATIONS

We find among the gifted the variety of capacities for social relations that we find among all children. Some get along easily with others, find pleasure in establishing new relationships, succeed easily, and feel very much at ease in any group. Others are not so interested in social relations, but have no special problems in relating to others. Finally, we have those who find it hard and painful to relate to others and who do not seem able to find their place in a social group. The counsellor should be on his guard when he encounters a gifted child from this last group. The reasons for the child's difficulties should be looked into, as well as the social structure of the group to which the child belongs and the one into which eventually he might be accelerated.

Another element related to social integration has to do with sex differences. In general, it is easier for a girl who is younger than her classmates to interact with the opposite sex than it is for a boy in a similar situation.

THE CHILD'S POINT OF VIEW

Johnny, in Grade 4, is in love with little Sophie who sits in the second row just before his wide-open and adoring eyes. Johnny has been identified as gifted, and the counsellor is considering the possibility of accelerating him and thus transferring him into Grade 5. Johnny is lucky, because his counsellor, before doing anything, decides to talk to him and finds out how important this relationship is. In the talk, Johnny also has an opportunity to express his social position in the class and the personal satisfaction he derives from it (on the socio-metric test Johnny appears to be one of the most popular children in his class). When the counsellor asks how Johnny feels about going into a higher class, Johnny emphatically refuses.

A child's willingness to separate from this group should be one of the counsellor's considerations when he makes decisions about acceleration. Sometimes, unfortunately, we decide "what's good" for the child and forget to ask him.

PARENTAL ATTITUDES

Counsellors dealing with gifted children very often come across the "pushy parent" phenomenon. It is of utmost importance that the counsellor realize how much the parent's attitude may be due to his own unfulfilled aspirations, or to frustrations in his personal life and a desire to compensate for them. In such cases, one of the obvious ways for parents to get their child ahead is to try to have him accelerated. School superintendents and counsellors are acquainted with this type of parent who frequently visits them and badgers them with a long list of good reasons for pushing the child up in the school grades.

As opposed to the "pushy parent," there are the parents who fear and reject the idea that their child may be special in any way. They are anxious at the thought that for any reason their child may be singled out, separated, pointed to, or dealt with differently than the average child. Their main concern is, "Let my child be like any other child."

So the question is what should the counsellor do about parental attitudes? If he feels, on the one hand, the "push" on the part of the parents and, on the other hand feels that the essential elements he weighs do not indicate acceleration, he has an obligation to enter into a counselling relationship with the parents. He will attempt to help them understand their own needs and the possible ill effects of their attitude on their child's needs. A similar approach is needed with the parents who want to hold the child back.

The counsellor's duty becomes one of informing the parents of the actual and important differences in needs which exists between their child and the average child. These parents must be made aware of how acceleration can be helpful to their child in the long run. However, the counsellor should be on his guard at all times and be aware of the parent's true feeling toward acceleration, because, in the final analysis, it is their child, and the decision remains their responsibility.

After all the basic precautions have been taken and the child can be safely accelerated with the parent's consent, the next step for the counsellor is to prepare the child and the new teacher. Of course, the counsellor has a continuing responsibility to maintain an interest in the child's adjustment and progress in his new class (in the form of a follow-up).

Grouping

Grouping is another type of special program for the gifted. It involves separating the gifted children as a group and working with them within the framework of a special curriculum adapted to their needs. Grouping can consist of two basic approaches: One is the creation of special schools to which only gifted students are admitted; the other is the provision of special classes for part-time activities of the gifted within the framework of the regular school.

In contrast to the positive trend of research on acceleration, research evidence on grouping is often contradictory. It is interesting to look into the series of studies which have been compiled and which yielded such contradictory results. On the one hand, strong evidence in favour of ability grouping for gifted children was shown in a review of the literature by Carter in 1960.[11] On the other hand, Passow and Goldberg, in 1961, studied the effects of grouping in a series of investigations over a period of two years and found very little difference in the achievement of gifted students placed in special groups and those who remained in their regular class.[12] How can we explain such contradictory findings? It is our feeling that grouping has often been used as a "magic concept." Gifted students are grouped and are taught material, not at their own class level, but at higher levels. It then becomes a matter of quantitatively increasing the teaching material for the gifted students. This is a fallacy. It is not "the what" which needs to change; it is "the how." There is a need to evaluate the quality of programs which are introduced in the special groups.

What are the advantages of grouping gifted children? The main advantage is the intellectual stimulation: a class consisting of extremely intelligent children only, demands of the teacher a state of constant alertness and a higher level of teaching. As we have said, the regular classroom has a level of teaching and a pace directed at the average student. The level of a class consisting exclusively of gifted students is obviously raised substantially. Consequently, the teacher's task is to deal with this change in level accordingly. This is by no means an easy task, and it demands much from the teacher. From the student's point of view, being put in a special group will help to solve many of his intellectual frustrations. We have mentioned already the gifted pupils' difficulties in being understood at their own level by their peers or in receiving their respect for unusual and bright ideas. We have seen their tendency to slowly estrange themselves from peer communication, at least at the intellectual level. In the special class they find a territory for free discussion and rich feedback. The teacher does not need to worry about the effect which a gifted pupil's intellectual escapades may create on the average group of students. On the contrary, the teacher can support and encourage the child to go as far as he will go. The gifted group will respond in kind by giving the teacher positive feedback and stimulation, and the whole process becomes a kind of collective enrichment.

A second advantage of grouping consists of providing richer and more rewarding social relations for the gifted. One of the gifted child's characteristics is his choosing of friends among either highly intelligent contemporaries or older children. He seems to be more interested in his peers' mental age than their chronological age. This advantage of grouping compensates for one of the disadvantages of acceleration, in that the gifted child does not find himself to be the youngest in a group of older children. He may be accelerated in a natural way without skipping classes.

An additional advantage which is related to both the intellectual and social aspects of grouping is that grouping provides a chance to compete with equals. The gifted child moves from a situation in which he is the best without exerting much effort to one in which, in order to be among the best, he must do his utmost. In a regular class, the gifted child learns quickly that almost independently of what he does, he is outstanding. Thus, he might develop the kind of superiority feelings that express: "I don't need to do anything in order to succeed."

Developing such an outlook on life does not give the child a chance to really test lifelike situations. In our culture, competition is one of the main elements of social living. The longer the child goes along without developing the realistic need to compete with others, the harder he will be hit by the bare reality of competition when he does have to face it. He may be so shocked that he may abandon all effort and decide to withdraw from any situation which presents this kind of threat. The grouping situation is a constant opportunity not only for competition, but also for collaboration with equals. The child may learn for the first time that he can be second, third, fifth, or even.the last one in the class and still be good. He gains insight into his own capabilities and limitations. Actually he is being cut to size. In a way, this should temper the fears of those who consider grouping the gifted as an act of favouritism.

Counselling the Intellectually Gifted Child

The advantage of competing with equals also has a negative aspect. The competition may be too severe. The student may feel over-burdened. Such a situation exists, for instance, in some special classes for the gifted in Tel-Aviv. A few teachers report that one of their most difficult problems is dealing with the pressure-cooker atmosphere the students create. The students themselves have established norms that are too demanding and unrealistic. It becomes the task of the teacher to keep his hand on the fast-beating pulse of the class and to ensure the delicate balance between co-operation and competition. One of the disadvantages of grouping is that it takes a very special teacher to cope with the various and difficult demands of a class of gifted students. Preparation for this task requires a different and specific pattern of training, in the same way as is required for other teachers who work with special groups, such as the mentally retarded.

Another danger inherent in grouping is the possibility that an artificial "intellectual ghetto" may be formed. The children belonging to the special group may feel isolated. The social gap between them and their average peers may be widened. Normal social life involves inter-action with a variety of people coming from different backgrounds, with their respective cultural norms and with a wide range of abilities and interests. The danger of the intellectual ghetto is that it can create an artificial world within a restricted range of possible social inter-actions. Even if the intellectual ghetto, by the high prestige it commands, may symbolize a golden cage, it is still a cage.

We may conclude from these points about grouping that the formation of positive and successful groups of gifted students needs the assistance of all the people involved. The superintendent of the school, the teachers, the parents, and even the children are essential partners in such a project. The counsellor can help in the co-ordination implementation and careful follow-up of grouping. What are the counsellor's main tasks?

There are six areas to which the alert counsellor should pay attention.

1 THE SCHOOL

The counsellor's obligations towards the school are those of a careful and thorough informer. His duty is to define clearly and impartially all the pros and cons of grouping as he sees them in the setting of the particular school. His remarks should be based on a good understanding of all the characteristics of the school, such as the social setting, the teaching staff available, the finances, and the possibilities for expansion into new programs. It is also his task to present to the school principal concrete evidence of the need for special grouping of the gifted students. He can do this by testing the children and forming an opinion as to the number of gifted children in the school and how well or how poorly their intellectual needs are being met. These investigations would ensure that his presentation of the specific grouping needs and his recommendation as to the type of grouping are based on realistic data.

2 THE GIFTED CHILD

The full and satisfying development of the gifted child according to his potential is, of course, what is at stake. The counsellor, therefore, must make sure that he knows who those children are, how they feel about their present situation in the classroom, their satisfactions, their frustrations, their problems, and what they would like to see changed. By interviewing the children, the counsellor can form a clear picture of their personal attitudes and feelings about being sealed out because of their intellectual uniqueness. He can discern their fears, their fantasies, and their misconceptions. He can clarify their doubts about the functioning and the purpose of grouping.

3 THE PARENTS

The counsellor's responsibility towards the parents is quite similar. Parents must be made aware of their real feelings and aspirations about their gifted child. There is a great variety of parental attitudes directed towards children with exceptional intellect. It is not always easy to accept giftedness as a fact. The counsellor must help the parents view this realistically. He can ask for the parents' co-operation in assisting the child to grow and develop into a well-adjusted human being, at peace with his superior skills. Both the parents and their child must be made to understand that participation in a special group is not an all-or-nothing decision.

Special groups are open systems. Any child who feels pressured, who cannot adjust, who feels inadequate, or who shows unhappiness for whatever reason, must feel free to bring his problem to the counsellor. The child must know that the opportunity to leave the special group and return to his normal classroom is an ever-present option open to him at all times. This is also true about returning to the special group at any time he may feel ready and willing to do so. Leaving the group does not mean failing or being a drop-out. A child who decides to leave, after discussing his reasons with the counsellor, must go with the productive awareness of new insights into his actions and capabilities. He has not lost the battle; he has gained a better understanding of how and where he functions at his very best.

4 THE TEACHERS

The fourth area of responsibility of the counsellor is his work with the teachers. The counsellor must keep close contact with the teachers in order to help them assist the gifted student in finding his place, be it in a special group or in a normal classroom. The counsellor must assist the teacher of a special group in delineating and organizing a good working group. Once this is functioning, teachers will constantly come across difficulties and dilemmas for which they will need a helping hand to cope with them or a friendly shoulder to cry on. A group of gifted children can sometimes be comprised of twenty non-conformists; this can be quite a problem to tackle, even for an expertly trained and competent teacher. Another danger which must be overcome is that of teachers who are subject-oriented and who deal with children as isolated brains; this could reinforce the intellectual ghettoism described previously.

5 THE SOCIAL SETTING

The counsellor can be of great assistance in opening up the ghetto by first of all reminding the teachers at all times not to forget the child behind the brain, the whole person behind the intellect. Secondly, he can outline ways of circumventing the isolation of children in special groups. There is no reason not to re-unite pupils of special groups with normal classes for activities like sports, music, drama, or arts and crafts. Social events can be organized to bring all the children together. This is what we meant when we specified the social setting as one of the counsellor's responsibilities. He must make sure to help create conditions which will favour opportunities for socialization among all pupils, gifted and average, and to prevent intellectual isolation from developing into an emotional and social isolation.

6 THE FOLLOW-UP

To ensure the fulfillment of these aims, the counsellor's long-standing duty is that of constantly keeping track of the development of the gifted pupils. This sixth area of responsibility of the counsellor means his preparation of a follow-up on each gifted pupil, in order to form a dynamic picture of the child which can serve later as the basis for further counselling for high school, college, or vocations.

Enrichment

Enrichment is nothing else than extracurricular grouping. The gifted children remain in the regular classrooms, and once or twice a week they participate in some special programs tailored to their needs. The main objective of such enrichment programs is the provision of additional intellectual stimulation to the gifted student. The material for enrichment is either subject matter from the regular school curriculum expanded and developed at higher levels, or from different subjects generally not taught in school.

At this point, we want to describe the advantages and the inconveniences of the special program at hand. Delineating the pros and cons of enrichment after those of grouping turns out to be somewhat paradoxical, because the very advantages of the one are inconveniences of the other and vice versa. For instance, the merit of enrichment lies mainly in that it prevents the development of intellectual ghettoism. Gifted children are not isolated, are not taught entirely different subject matter, and do not form their relationships separately. The normal classroom retains the whole range of variety of children, and the peer group includes both gifted and average children. The gifted children are not deprived of the opportunity for greater development according to their ability. But this very advantage of enrichment incorporates all the inconveniences, as we previously discussed, of being gifted and remaining in one's normal classroom. Enrichment in conjunction with the normal classroom attendance is helpful, but it incorporates some dangers. One of these is the science bias. Subjects chosen for the programs are almost exclusively in the exact sciences. In general, such programs are organized by universities, where special classes in mathematcs, chemistry, electronics, computers, or what-have-you are presented by faculty members of various university departments.

These programs enjoy high prestige because of the locality – the campus – and because of such rich facilities as laboratories, computers, and videotapes. A multitude of such programs exist all over the world; they are generally very popular in spite of the fact that there are almost no research data on their possible benefit. There is no doubt that children who are interested in the programs enjoy positive enrichment. However, there is not only an intellectual, but also a "snob appeal" in such programs. For many parents, having their twelve-year-old child going to university becomes a favourite conversation piece devoid of modesty, to say the least. In the author's experience, many children who have participated in the programs have become boastful and snobbish with their peers. Hints like "This afternoon I can't join the gang; I'm going to the university" do not always fall into the most appreciative ears. It is a pity that such university programs do not include the participation of a counsellor who can be sensitive to these attitudes and work with the children to help them neutralize the negative effects.

The question arises: How can one create enrichment programs which offer all the advantages of added stimulation without the disadvantages such as the science bias, the snob appeal, or the lack of a counsellor? As one answer to the question, we present below an enrichment program for gifted children which tries to combine some of the advantages of grouping as well as those of enrichment. This program involves not only the gifted child, but also his parents and the community as a whole.

A community-based enrichment program for gifted children

How does one create a well-rounded enrichment program which leaves the child in his environment and brings him close to his parents and to his community? Such an experiment has been made in Israel with the purpose of achieving a joint parent-child community enrichment program for all gifted children. The main objectives of the experiment were:

1 To take enrichment programs out of the university setting and bring them to the community of the child.

2 To design a program for the children of the community as a whole, thereby transcending barriers between neighbourhood schools.

3 To create, under professional guidance, a co-operative effort between parent and child which would enrich their mutual relationship.

The reason for taking enrichment programs out of the university setting are clear. On the one hand there are the negative effects of snob appeal on both the children and their parents. On the other hand there are the parents who are against sending their children to such programs for fear of making them even more "special." Another problem involves transportation to the campus from the various home neighbourhoods of the children.

In Israel, as in most countries of the western world, schools are organized in neighbourhoods, which reflect the differences in the socio-economic level of their inhabitants. The regional divisions of the schools create barriers, which, in turn, limit the possibilities for community involvement. Children from disadvantaged neighbourhoods have very few opportunities to participate in co-operative activities and to exploit their talents in a collective effort. It is possible that the use of extra-curricular programs for talented children of the community as a whole may diminish the barriers created by such divisions as well as ethnic and class-status differences. It has been hypothesized that a co-operative community effort in an interesting and enjoyable project might possibly effect a tremendous amount of community interaction, not only among the children themselves, but also among the parents.

The parents of gifted children frequently face puzzling questions in relation to them. Very often the parents find it difficult to answer their children's many questions. They worry that their children are different from others. They are disturbed when their children do not take part in other children's games and prefer to spend their time reading or conducting "dangerous experiments." And then what can be more disturbing to the parents than when the child does not study what is required of him in school, complains that school is boring, and in some cases wants to stop attending school altogether. Many a time a distressed parent, feeling unable to handle the child's problems, expects the school to come up with the right solution and, if possible, with all the solutions. Schools, however, are usually not equipped with either the professional manpower or the curricula required to handle these problems. One way of helping parents to understand their gifted child better and to cope more effectively with him is to transform them from passive "help-seekers" into active participants in effective work with gifted children. In the Israeli community programs, parents became partners in all the stages of implementation of the program; they participated actively in the planning, the teaching, and the administration.

What was done to get the program started? First, teachers were informed of the program and its purpose. They were asked for helpful ideas and for active participation in the identification process. The Terman approach was used, and each teacher was aksed to nominate three pupils whom he or she regarded as the most intelligent in the class. (As we mentioned earlier, teacher nomination has some drawbacks, but these were consciously overlooked in the application of this particular project.) Forty classes were involved and, therefore, 120 children were nominated.

The next step was to approach the parents. They were invited to a general meeting and presented with the main ideas of the program. The meeting was divided into two parts, during the first of which the difficulties of gifted children and accepted methods of dealing with them at home and at school were described as background information. The staff then suggested to the parents a program in which the parents would participate actively in both organization and pedagogy. Then the question of subjects to be taught was introduced. It was made clear that the program was not intended to compete with the existing school curriculum, but rather to introduce children to the extent and depth of the world around them. A humanistic program was devised to present the children with subject matter to which they were not exposed directly in the schools, but which they are faced with in their day-to-day life. The subjects were:

1 *Psychology.* This subject was chosen because it is close to a person's daily life and is of major importance in the understanding of all human interaction.

2 *Dramatic expression.* This was chosen because it provides novel means for the expression of feelings and thoughts in a playful way.

3 *Architecture.* This was chosen to help the children to become sensitive to ecology and aesthetics.

4 *Journalism.* This was chosen as one of the most widely used forms of mass communication in our society.

5 *Drawing and painting.* This was chosen because of the possibilities for self-expression when children are taught in an open and encouraging manner.

6 *Game planning.* This was chosen in order to enable the children to understand the principles of games theory, plan its stages, and determine by themselves strategies, all of which deepen the pleasure derived from the games they take part in and invent.

All of these subjects are of interest to anyone, child or adult, living in the contemporary world. Still, they are not part of the usual school curriculum and, therefore, there can be no competition between the school program and the enrichment program.

During the second part of the evening the parents were divided into small discussion groups. Parents were invited to exchange questions, comments, and opinions with other parents and with the two psychologists attending each group. During the discussions volunteers were requested for administering the program. There was more response than needed to the call for volunteers. Teachers for most of the workshops were also found among the parents, in spite of the expressed concern about lack of expertise.

The next step was a campaign to inform the children of the program and the content and goals of the workshops. It turned out, however, that to explain to a third-grader what a workshop in psychology has to offer is not an exceptionally easy task. The information sheet distributed to the children had to be understandable to children in Grade Three and still be attractive enough for the older ones in Grade Five. Once completed, the information sheet was sent by mail to each child. By the time the workshops were formed, each contained from twelve to fifteen children.

Before actual work started with the children, parents attended guidance programs in which they were prepared for their roles as teachers. In spite of the fact that parents had a professional background in the subject they were teaching (for example, the workshop in journalism was run by a father who was a journalist), some of the parents showed great apprehension about their ability to cope with this group of exceptional children. The main purpose of the guidance workshop was to alleviate these fears.

Then the meetings of the children's workshops began. These took place once a week for three months, each meeting lasting approximately two hours. The atmosphere was free and receptive. The children were given the opportunity to contribute to, and influence the course content of, the workshop. A counsellor and two volunteer parents attended each workshop in order to observe and, if necessary, provide support and guidance to the teacher. At the end of each meeting the children were requested to evaluate the session on a scale from one to five. The results of these evaluations were totalled and offered to each teacher. This direct feedback enabled the children to influence the role of their teacher. Field trips were organized to various places of interest such as museums, printing plants, and a psychology laboratory.

Since this community-based enrichment program for gifted children was not intended as a research project, no systematic measurements were included. It was possible, however, to assess some of the impact of the program on all participants, children and parents alike. The children's ratings were altogether favourable, and almost all of them showed willingness and enthusiasm to continue with such a program during the following academic year. The parents' reports were also positive. At their meetings, parents described how the children reported their excitement and pleasure in the workshops. Most importantly, parents were happy to report the richer interaction between themselves and their children which stemmed from the shared activities in the program. They all expressed their readiness to continue the involvement in joint parent-child intellectual ventures. However, since this was only a sort of "pilot study," a future program organized along these lines should include systematic research as well. The results of such research could become the guideline for the implementation of similar programs in different communities.

What conclusions can be drawn from the discussion about different types of special programs? The main conclusion is that one cannot say which program would be the best for all gifted children. Some programs are good for some children, and some children can live without any special program at all. In deciding which program would fit any particular child, all the elements discussed in this chapter should be taken into consideration.

8 The Disadvantaged Gifted

Up to now our book has tried to cover the scope of the needs, problems, and characteristics of the gifted population as a whole. But there is an important segment of that population which has not been touched upon at all; this is the disadvantaged gifted. The term "disadvantaged gifted" encompasses a great variety of terminologies. Articles have been written about the economically disadvantaged, the culturally handicapped, the culturally diverse, the educationally disadvantaged, and the culturally different. Although each of these categories can, and often has been, defined by different authors, there are some characteristics which are shared by all of these groups.

What these groups have in common is that, because of the environmental conditions – socio-economic status, a foreign culture, being part of a minority group, or living in a depressed area – they cannot utilize their intellectual potential to the fullest. This is cretainly true for *all* deprived children, not simply the gifted among them. The fact that the intellectually gifted child needs more stimulation than the child of average intelligence causes the gifted child to be, in a way, even more handicapped.

In Chapter 2 we saw how disproportionate the number of professional parents was in Terman's sample of gifted children. There is no doubt that children of families in this category enjoy good schooling, have stimulating working conditions at home, a variety of educational toys and books, and parents who value and encourage intellectual achievement. All of these conditions are lacking in the home of the disadvantaged gifted child.

A gifted child in an underprivileged home who has the same high potential as a gifted child from a professional family is so severely handicapped by his living conditions that, without help, he will rarely be able to fulfill his intellectual potential. As Ausubel noted in 1967, early identification of giftedness in these cases is crucial, for if an organism is deprived of necessary stimulation during a critical period, restricted developmental possibilities ensue.[1] At this point it is impossible to assess numerically the tremendous loss of talent among the disadvantaged gifted, but it is certain that the loss is impressive.

The identification of, and special programs and counselling for, the gifted, which we described in Chapter 7 become even more essential for a disadvantaged gifted child. The general living conditions of underprivileged children as a whole bring up many questions as to the problematic family relations, home environment, and school systems to which they are exposed. This being the case, it is no wonder that very little attention is paid to the gifted among them. The weight of the main handicapping factors is so important that this must be counterbalanced first. This in itself is a huge job and one with which professionals have had very little success up to now, as can be seen from the extensive professional literature on the subject. Difficulty does not mean impossibility and there is no reason why special attention should not be paid to the disadvantaged gifted; it is an attention to which the child is entitled from the social and human points of view. For the counsellor who works with underprivileged children, we shall present some ideas which might help to foster the element of giftedness in this population. This assistance should be based on a basic understanding of the handicaps limiting these children.

Figure 8 presents in schematic form some of the basic handicaps confronting the disadvantaged as a whole. The gifted among them are

Fig. 8   BASIC HANDICAPS OF DISADVANTAGED CHILDREN

	DISADVANTAGED CHILDREN
1 Relation to dominant culture	Antagonistic; leading to frustrations
2 Family structure	Great number of children and less individual attention to each child; more broken families
3 Future planning	Generally, short term "get now what you can"
4 Quality of education	Generally poor
5 Attitudes toward education	Generally negative "doesn't lead you anywhere"
6 Intellectual stimulation	Few books, few games, few cultural stimuli (museums, concerts, etc.)
7 Language	Poor; use of slang
8 Physical conditions	Overcrowded homes; health and nutrition poor
9 Interaction with adults	Sparse
10 Relation to authority	Rebellious

limited in addition by problems of non-recognition and the ensuing lack of special programs.

The disadvantaged gifted we have talked about up to now are basically those who come from the lower socio-economic strata, be it from depressed areas or from a foreign culture. There is, however, another group of disadvantaged gifted who come from about 50 per cent of the total population; these are the gifted females. In their case the term "disadvantaged" does not relate to socio-economic or ethnic backgrounds, but rather to the specific and restricting attitudes and expectations society has bestowed upon them.

Let us turn now to this group of disadvantaged: the women. Although intelligence is equally distributed among the sexes, women do not realize their high intellectual potential as frequently as men. There is a tremendous "woman talent loss" which is felt especially in the occupations requiring above-average and high ability. In the Terman study, it was found that the proportion of gifted boys and girls in primary schools was more or less equal. In his sample of high school students, the proportion was 160 boys to 100 girls. Finally, in his follow-up well into adulthood, Terman found that when the average age was 44, half of the women in his gifted sample were housewives with no outside employment. While 13.8 per cent of the men had a doctoral degree, only 5 per cent of the women had achieved this academic level.

Today, women do go into higher education more than they did thirty years ago, but they still receive fewer degrees than men.[2] Even in those areas considered "female fields" (with the exception of nursing), the proportion of degrees awarded to women decreases as the level of the degree increases.

The fact is that we find more men achieving successfully even in those activities stereotyped as "female fields," such as the fine and applied arts, the humanities, education, and even the culinary and fashion world. And when we examine achievement in science, the imbalance is much greater.

Why is it that gifted women are a minority, that women who can produce intellectually and artistically constitute such a small proportion of the female population?

The problem of the gifted woman is not as inherent in her nature as in her relationship to a society which accepts her only on certain conditions. And if she attempts to gain society's acceptance by fulfilling all these conditions she has an overwhelming task. A woman can go into any career she desires, as long as, at the same time, she manages to be a good wife, a good mother, good-looking, good-tempered, well-dressed, well-groomed, and unaggressive. These are the entrance charges for the approval of other men and women. But looking backwards, nobody actually expected George Eliot to be a beauty; nobody worried about Jeanne d'Arc's haircut. Emily Dickinson was not scorned for being childless; and nobody urged Marie Curie to dye her hair.

Komarovsky's classic paper shows the consistency of role conflict in women and the attempts to make themselves more desirable by hiding abilities.[3] Horner's paper reveals the same feelings of frustration, hostility, bitterness, and of being shut out of participation in the competitive occupational spheres. She found that a critical barrier to women's success in competitive academic or occupational roles lies in their internal fear of success. She termed this "the motive to avoid success."[4] An example of this can be seen in the dramatic difference in the answers to the question: "Do you think of yourself as an artist?" which art students were asked in an interview. Sixty-seven per cent of the women said "No," while 66 per cent of the men replied "Yes." When the students were asked if they would rate their own work as particularly unique or good in comparison to the work of others at the Institute, 40 per cent of the men, but only 17 per cent of the women felt that their work was of superior quality.[5] It is a fact that our culture is male-oriented and that a woman in a dominant position is regarded as a threat to the male ego.

As we can see, society has predetermined what woman's role is to be, and girls are reared to be conforming and dependent. Gifted woman face many additional difficulties in attaining eminence in a career, such as interrupted education, lack of mobility, less specialization, or getting a late start. The female sex-role does not allow much independence in our culture.

But even in our culture, there are very significant differences in the numbers of women who enter what are considered to be male-dominated professions. Russia is the only striking exception to the rule, although France and England have a much higher percentage of women in "masculine" professions than the United States.

Evelyne Sullerot noticed some of the differences between four western countries in the percentage of females in "masculine" professions.[6] In Medicine, Russia led the field with 76 per cent, with England showing 25 per cent, France, 22 per cent and the United States, 6 per cent. Russia again led in Law with 38 per cent of the women, but France was second with 19 per cent, followed by England with 4 per cent and the United States with 3. In Engineering, Russia had 37 per cent, followed again by France with 3.7 per cent. The United States had only .07 per cent in the profession and was trailed by England with only .06 per cent.

It is curious to note how low the percentage of women in these professions seems to be in the United States. It is particularly curious because of the stereotype of American culture as being matriarchal. On the other hand, perhaps the state of affairs revealed by these figures might be one of the basic factors in the rebirth of the women's liberation movement in the United States.

There is currently a definite change taking place in society, and the emphasis on the supportive role of women is diminishing. Society is beginning to view women as individuals, but the process is slow. Every modern gifted female should be encouraged and be able to achieve what Simone de Beauvoir calls the "individual personality," that is, the ability to shift the proportions of her life and to evolve from exclusive femaleness towards the fulfillment of a wider personality. Parents and educators who are charged with the responsibility of raising and training girls find themselves faced with a dilemma. What kinds of women do they want to produce? Does intellectuality in women develop only at the expense of their femininity? Does a woman really need to be passive and dependent in order to be sexually attractive to men or to be a good mother? We shall present some guidelines for the counsellor at the end of this chapter.

We have already seen that there are some gifted children who are handicapped by the very structure of our society. Obviously these children have the same right to be helped to develop their potential as do gifted children as a whole. In order to help these children, one has first to be aware of them, or in other words, one has first to identify them.

As we have seen, identification is a rather complex process; it becomes even more complicated when one deals with the underprivileged. One of the reasons for this is the fact that, generally, the very conditions of the underprivileged segment of society are not very favourable to the search for and identification of the gifted. To start with, school systems in underprivileged areas are often inadequately staffed; they lack professional and educational manpower. Even when counsellors and psychologists are at hand, they are so overburdened with the various and pressing problems of this population that they seldom have the time to deal with the identification of giftedness. We are aware and recognize that the day-to-day problems of these schools push aside the question of "talent loss." It might also be true that counsellors and psychologists, who mostly come from middle-class backgrounds, may be less attentive and aware of signs of giftedness in this population. Smith and Prindle maintain that teachers of the disadvantaged tend to write more negative than positive comments on cumulative records, regardless of measured intelligence or academic achievement.[7]

In spite of these difficulties, there is no doubt in our mind that identification of the disadvantaged gifted child is crucial from the perspectives of both society and the individual child. Is the process of identifying the disadvantaged gifted child different from the process which we have described for the gifted population as a whole? It certainly is different, and it is based much more on information gathering than on the classic intelligence tests, the observational methods, and the collaboration of teachers, parents, and peers which we described. Teachers should be made aware of the necessity for an active lookout for signs of giftedness among the disadvantaged. Tests with no time limits could help to find those children who have a high potential but not enough motivation to work in standardized time limits. Observation outside the classroom can help to discover aspects of giftedness which are not expressed in the normal class situation. This is an even more important factor in establishing the criteria for the identification of the disadvantaged gifted than for other groups of the gifted, because data gathered in academic settings may be biased by the negative attitudes which the child may have developed towards school. Sato's excellent paper presents many techniques for identifying the disadvantaged gifted child.[8]

But, of course, identifying these children is only the first step. Specific action should come next. Different approaches are being devised and tried out. Most of these are geared towards helping disadvantaged children in general and not the gifted in particular. Some are directed towards enrichment in the school; others try to enrich the home environment of the disadvantaged by working with the parents.

A more extreme approach to this problem was taken in a project for disadvantaged gifted children in Israel. Some Israelis educators refused to accept the proposition that children who spent their early years in disadvantaged social and cultural conditions could not be helped to overcome these handicaps and be encouraged and directed towards better behavioural patterns and higher levels of achievement.[9] In specially created boarding schools for disadvantaged gifted pupils these educators organized special enrichment curricula which showed very positive results in a six-year follow-up. The children were accepted into the program at the Grades 8–9 level. Almost all the gifted disadvantaged from these boarding schools finished high school successfully and passed their matriculation examinations. Only 45 per cent of the gifted children from the same socio-economic background who stayed in their original classrooms did so.

This example shows what one kind of special program can achieve in terms of fostering educational achievement in the disadvantaged. More importantly, perhaps, the positive results of this enrichment program, which starts at the high school level, point to the fact that the destructive powers of underprivileged living conditions are not irreversible. In other words, although theoretically it is easier to start as early as possible, it is never too late to start a good thing.

The problem of the disadvantaged female is very different. The main question here is not related to identification but to changing the attitudes of parents and teachers. The role of the counsellor in this situation is to come to grips with a new attitude towards women and shed social sexual labels, so that the active, dominant, independent qualities of the intellectual girl can lead her to the fulfillment of her abilities. The question is not that of educating women in the same way as men or differently from them. Instead, education must evolve for each girl on the basis of her needs and goals as a person. Up to now, society has constantly made assumptions as to what girls should become. Today it is the main role of counsellors, educators, and parents to allow girls the freedom to choose the best path for themselves. Parents should be helped to accept, for example, the fact that their little girl has the potential to become a good scientist. They must be helped to accept in her the qualities of dominance, independence, and active striving which appear to be requisites for good analytic thinking. In short, parents must be dissuaded from discouraging their little girls, and this can only happen through a radical change in the conventions concerning appropriate behaviour for the sexes.

The point of this whole book is to show how difficult the task is of fostering gifted children in our society. The United States Commissioner of Education pointed out, in his report in 1972, that of 2 to 2½ million gifted children in the United States only 4 per cent find adequate help in schools; the situation is probably not too different elsewhere. Certainly among the chosen few, the disadvantaged gifted constitute an infinitesimal number. As we have seen, society in general, and the educational establishment in particular, very often have biased, misinformed, or uninformed views of the gifted. This is the situation which leads to non-recognition and neglect for most of the gifted, and the disadvantaged gifted in particular. We do not live under the illusion that the counsellor has the power to effect significant changes in society's approach. His main contribution can be made in the modest but indispensable creation of conditions for awareness, recognition, and assistance. If this book helps some counsellors to deal more effectively with and for some gifted children, and if it helps some parents to understand more clearly their beloved, but bewildering, gifted offspring, we shall consider our effort worth while.

Notes to Chapter 1

1 Alfred North Whitehead, "Preface" to W. B. Donham, *Business Adrift* (1931), p. 6.
2 Alvin Toffler, *Future Shock* (1970).
3 Cyril L. Burt, "The Gifted Child," in F. Berenday (ed.), *The Gifted Child* (1962).
4 Ernst Kretchmer, *The Psychology of Men of Genius* (1951).
5 W. Russell Brain, *Some Reflections On Genius* (1960).
6 John W. Gardner, *Excellence: Can We Be Equal and Excellent Too?* (1961), p. 17.
7 Lewis M. Terman, "The Discovery and Encouragement of Exceptional Talent" (1954), p. 12.
8 D. L. Thistlewhite, "The Conservation of Intellectual Talent" (1958).
9 William James, "Stanford's Ideal Destiny" (Founder's Day Address, 1906 in Memories and Studies [New York: Longmans Green & Co., 1934]).
10 Joseph L. French (ed.), *Educating the Gifted* (1959).
11 Harvey C. Lehman, *Age and Achievement* (1953).

Notes to Chapter 2

1 Lewis M. Terman, "Intelligence and Its Measurement" (1921), p. 132.
2 Edward L. Thorndike, "Intelligence and Its Measurement" (1921), p. 124.
3 Stephen S. Colvin, "Intelligence and Its Measurement" (1921), p. 143.
4 Rudolph Pintner, "Intelligence and Its Measurement" (1921), p. 149.
5 T. Robert Miles, "On Defining Intelligence" (1957).
6 W. J. Meyer and G. C. Thompson, "Sex Differences in the Distribution of Teacher Approval and Disapproval Among Sixth Grade Children" (1959).
7 John C. Gowan and George D. Demos, *The Education and Guidance of the Ablest* (1964).
8 J. J. Conger, *Adolescence and Youth* (1973).
9 Francis A. Steward, "Measuring Intelligence" in Anne Anastasi, *Differential Psychology* (1958).
10 Hans J. Eysenck, *Uses and Abuses of Psychology* (1959).
11 Allison Davis, "Socio-economic Influences Upon Children's Learning" (1951).
12 Jacob W. Getzels and Philip W. Jackson, *Creativity and Intelligence* (1962).
13 Kauro Yamamoto, "Effects of Restriction of Range and Test Unreliability on Correlation Between Measures of Intelligence and Creative Thinking" (1965).
14 S. B. Crockenberg, "Creativity Tests: Boon or Boondoggle for Education" (1972).

Notes to Chapter 3

1 Lewis M. Terman, *Mental and Physical Traits of a Thousand Gifted Children* (1925), p. 169.
2 *Ibid.*, p. 437.
3 *Ibid.*, p. 439.
4 Terman, "The Discovery and Encouragement of Exceptional Talent" (1954).
5 Terman, *The Promise of Youth* (1930), p. 30.
6 J. C. Jacobs, "Teacher Attitudes Towards Gifted Children" (1972).
7 R. George Pohl, "Teacher Nomination of Intellectually Gifted Children in the Primary Grades" (1970).

8 H. Herbert Hughes and Harold D. Converse, "Characteristics of the Gifted: A Case for a Sequel to Terman's Study" (1962).
9 Frank Laycock and John S. Caylor, "Physique of Gifted Children and Their Less Gifted Siblings" (1964).
10 Edward C. Frierson, "Upper and Lower Status Gifted Children: A Study of Differences" (1965).
11 Terman, *Mental and Physical Traits of a Thousand Gifted Children* (1925), p. 39.
12. Jacob W. Getzels and J. T. Dillon, "Giftedness and the Education of the Gifted" (1973).
13 L. Erlenmeyer Kimling and L. F. Jarvick, "Genetics and Intelligence: A Review" (1963).
14 Elizabeth M. Drews, "A Four Year Study of 150 Gifted Adolescents" (1957).
15 Leta S. Hollingsworth, *Children Above 180 I.Q.* (1942).
16 Anne Roe, "A Psychologist Examines 64 Eminent Scientists" (1952).
17 Donald W. MacKinnon, "The Nature and Nurture of Creative Talent" (1962).
18 Frank X. Barron, *Creative Person and Creative Process* (1969).
19 J. P. Guilford, "Three Faces of Intellect" (1959).
20 S. B. Crockenberg, "Creativity Tests: Boon or Boondoggle for Education" (1972).
21 George Erickson, "The Predictive Validity of a Battery of Creative Thinking Tests and Peer Nominations Among University of Minnesota High School Seniors Seven Years Later" (1966).
22 Crockenberg, *op. cit.*

Notes to Chapter 4

1 John C. Flanagan, "Project Talent: Preliminary Findings" (1967).
2 J. R. Warren and P. A. Heist, "Personality Attributes of Gifted College Students" (1960).
3 E. Edward D'Heurle, "Personality, Intellectual and Achievement Patterns of Gifted Children" (1959).
4 Lewis M. Terman, *Mental and Physical Traits of a Thousand Gifted Children* (1925).
5 W. M. Bart, "The Effect of Interest on Horizontal Decalage of the Stage of Forward Operations" (1971).
6 Donald W. MacKinnon, "The Nature and Nurture of Creative Talent" (1962).
7 Frank X. Barron, *Artists in the Making* (1972).

Notes to Chapter 5

1 Kelmer M. L. Pringle, *Able Misfits* (1970).
2 Irene H. Impelizzeri, D. L. Barr, and I. E. Conney, "An Investigation of Scholastic Functioning of 4875 High Ability Secondary Students in New York City" (1965).
3 R. H. McGillivray, "Differences in Home Background Between High Achieving and Low Achieving Gifted Children" (1964).
4 Merville C. Shaw, "Note on Parental Attitudes Toward Independence Training and the Academic Achievement of Their Children" (1964).
5 Norma J. Groth, "Differences in Parental Environment Needed for Degree Achievement for Gifted Men and Women" (1971).

6 Robert C. Nichols, "Parental Attitudes of Intelligent Adolescents and Creativity of Their Children" (1964).
7 Avner Ziv, "The Self Image of Underachieving Gifted Children" (1975).
8 C. E. Osgood *et al.*, *The Measurement of Meaning* (1957).
9 Merville C. Shaw and John T. McCuen, "The Onset of Academic Underachievement in Bright Children" (1960).
10 Ludwig Weiss, "Underachievement — Empirical Studies" (1972).
11. Lewis M. Terman, *Mental and Physical Traits of a Thousand Gifted Children* (1925).
12 Anne Roe, "A Psychologist Examines 64 Eminent Scientists" (1952).
13 Donald W. MacKinnon, "The Nature and Nurture of Creative Talent" (1962).
14 Victor and Mildred G. Goertzel, *Cradles of Eminence* (1962).
15 Harvey A. Grace and Nancy L. Booth, "Is the Gifted Child a Socially Isolate?" (1958).
16 Avner Ziv, *Psychological Aspects of Education* (1975).
17 K. L. and W. J. Grazin, "Peer Group Choice as a Device for Screening Intellectually Gifted Children" (1969).
18 James S. Coleman, *The Adolescent Society* (1962).
19 Harriet E. O'Shea, "Friendship and the Intellectually Gifted Child" (1960).

Notes to Chapter 6

1 Mary N. Meeker, *The Structure of Intellect: Its Uses and Implications* (1969).
2 Catherine B. Bruch, "A Creativity Score From the Stanford-Binet and Its Applications" (1969).
3 Carlo Scarpellini, "Riverlazioni sugli alumni intellectualmente dotati: il guidizio scolastico e psicologico" (1967).
4 Lewis M. Terman, *Mental and Physical Traits of a Thousand Gifted Children* (1925), p. 21.
5 Avner Ziv, "Children's Behavior Problems as Viewed by Teachers, Psychologists and Children" (1970).
6 Samuel R. Laycock. *Gifted Children* (1957).
7 Gertrude H. Hildreth, *Introduction to the Gifted* (1966).
8 J. C. Jacobs, "Teacher Attitudes Towards Gifted Children" (1972).
9 R. L. Cornish, "Parents' Teachers' and Pupils' Perception of the Gifted Child's Ability" (1968).
10 Hildreth, *op. cit.*
11 Willard Abraham, *Common Sense About Gifted Children* (1958).
12 K. L. and W. J. Grazin, "Peer Group Choice as a Device for Screening Intellectually Gifted Children" (1969).
13 Catharine M. Cox, *The Early Mental Traits of 300 Geniuses* (1926).
14 Anne Roe, "A Psychologist Examines 64 Eminent Scientists" (1952).
15 Donald W. MacKinnon, "The Nature and Nurture of Creative Talent" (1962).

Notes to Chapter 7

1 M. F. Shiman, *Individual Learning* (1970).
2 Jacob W. Getzels and J. T. Dillon, "Giftedness and the Education of the Gifted" (1973).
3 Miriam L. Goldberg, *Research on the Talented* (1965).
4 Lewis M. Terman and Melita H. Oden, *The Gifted Child Grows Up* (1947).

5 J. H. Monderer, "An Evaluation of Nebraska Program of Early Entrance to Elementary School (1954).
6 Noemi Weisman, "Early School Admission of Gifted Children" (1972).
7 Sidney L. Pressey, "Educational Acceleration: Occasional Procedure or Major Issue?" (1962).
8 Terman and Oden, *op. cit.*, p. 275
9 Walter B. Barbe and Manfred Adler, "William Sidis: On Child Prodigy" (1972).
10 *Ibid.*, p. 84.
11 H. D. Carter, "Gifted Children" (1960).
12 A Harvey Passow and Miriam L. Goldberg, "The Talented Youth Project: A Progress Report" (1961).

Notes to Chapter 8

1 David P. Ausubel, "How Reversible Are the Cognitive and Motivational Effects of Cultural Deprivation?" (1967).
2 Cynthia F. Epstein, *A Woman's Place: Options and Limits in Professional Careers* (1970).
3 Mirra Komarowsky, "Cultural Traditions and Sex Roles" (November, 1946).
4 Martina Horner, "The Motives to Avoid Success and Changing Aspirations of College Women" (1970).
5 Frank X. Barron, *Artists in the Making* (1972).
6 Evelyne Sullerot, *Woman, Society and Change* (1971).
7 P. G. Smith and V. T. Prindle, "The Culturally Disadvantaged Pupil on Cumulative Record" (1969).
8 I. S. Sato, "The Culturally Different Child — the Dawning of His Day" (1974).
9 Moshe Smilansky and David Nevo, *Secondary Boarding for Gifted Students From Disadvantaged Strata* (1971).

Bibliography

ABRAHAM, WILLARD. *Common Sense About Gifted Children.* New York: Harper, 1958.

AUSUBEL, DAVID P. "How Reversible are the Cognitive and Motivational Effects of Cultural Deprivation?" in PASSOW, A. HARVEY (ed.) *Education of the Disadvantaged.* New York: Holt Rinehart & Winston, 1967.

BARBE, WALTER B., and ADLER, MANFRED. "William Sidis: On Child Prodigy," in HAUCK, BARBARA B., and FREEHILL, MAURICE F. (eds.). *The Gifted — Case Studies.* Dubuque: William C. Brown Company, 1972.

BARRON, FRANK X. *Creative Person and Creative Process.* New York: Holt Rinehart & Winston, 1969.

————. *Artists in the Making.* New York: Seminar Press, 1972.

BART, W. M. "The Effect of Interest on Horizontal Decalage of the Stage of Forward Operations," *Journal of Psychology,* LXXXVIII (1971), 142–46.

BRAIN, W. RUSSELL. *Some Reflections on Genius.* London: Figler, 1960.

————. *Psychology of Genius.* London, Figler, 1962.

BRUCH, CATHERINE B. "A Creativity Score from the Stanford-Binet and Its Applications," *CEC Selected Convention Papers.* Arlington, Va.: The Council for Exceptional Children (1969), pp. 1–4.

BURKS, BARBARA S., JENSON, DORTHA W., and TERMAN, LEWIS M. *The Promise of Youth: Follow-Up Studies of a Thousand Gifted Children.* (*Genetic Studies of Genius,* ed. Lewis M. Terman, Vol III) Stanford: Stanford University Press, 1925.

BURT, CYRIL L. "The Inheritance of Mental Ability," *American Psychologist,* XIII (1958), 1–15.

————. "The Gifted Child," in BERENDAY F. (ed.). *The Gifted Child.* New York: Harcourt Brace, 1962.

CARTER, H. D. "Gifted Children," in HARRIS, CHESTER W. (ed.). *Encyclopedia of Educational Research.* New York: The Macmillan Company, 1960.

COLEMAN, JAMES W. *The Adolescent Society.* New York: Free Press of Glencoe, 1962.

COLVIN, STEPHEN S. "Intelligence and Its Measurement," *Journal of Educational Psychology,* XII (1921), 141–44.

CONGER, JOHN J. *Adolescence and Youth.* New York: Harper & Row, 1973.

COOPERSMITH, STANLEY. *The Antecedents of Self-Esteem.* San Francisco: W. H. Freeman & Company, 1967.

CORNISH, R. L. "Parents' Teachers' and Pupils' Perception of the Gifted Child's Ability," *Gifted Child Quarterly,* XII (1968), 14–17.

COX, CATHARINE M. *The Early Mental Traits of Three Hundred Geniuses.* (*Genetic Studies of Genius,* ed. LEWIS M. TERMAN, Vol. II.) Stanford: Stanford University Press, 1926.

CROCKENBERG, S. B. "Creativity Tests: Boon or Boondoggle for Education," *Review of Educational Research,* XLII (1972), 27–45.

DAVIS, ALLISON. "Socio-economic Influences Upon Children's Learning," *Understanding the Child,* XX (1951), 10–16.

D'HEURLE, E. EDWARD. "Personality, Intellectual and Achievement Patterns of Gifted Children," *Psychological Monographs,* LXXXIII (1959), No. 13.

DREWS, ELIZABETH M. "A Four Year Study of 150 Gifted Adolescents," Mimeographed report presented to American Psychological Association, 1957.

EPSTEIN, CYNTHIA F. *A Woman's Place: Options and Limits in Professional Corners.* Berkeley: University of California Press, 1970.

ERICKSON, GEORGE. "The Predictive Validity of a Battery of Creative Thinking Tests and Peer Nomination Among University of Minnesota High School Seniors Seven Years Later." Unpublished Master's research, University of Minnesota, 1966.

ERLENMEYER KIMLING, L., and JARVICK, L. F. "Genetics and Intelligence: A Review," *Science*, CXLII (1963), 1477–79.

EYSENCK, HANS J. *Uses and Abuses of Psychology.* London: Pelican Books, 1959.

FLANAGAN, JOHN C. "Project Talent: Preliminary Findings." Mimeographed. Pittsburg University, 1967.

FRENCH, JOSEPH L. (ed.). *Educating the Gifted.* New York: Holt Rinehart & Winston, 1959.

FRIERSON, EDWARD C. "Upper and Lower Status Gifted Children: A Study of Differences," *Exceptional Children*, XXXII (1965), 83–90.

GALTON, SIR FRANCIS. *Hereditary Genius.* London: Macmillan & Co., 1869.

GARDNER, JOHN W. *Excellence: Can We Be Equal and Excellent Too?* New York: Harper & Row, 1961.

GETZELS, JACOB W., and JACKSON, PHILIP W. *Creativity and Intelligence.* New York: John Wiley and Sons, 1962.

GETZELS, JACOB W., and DILLON, J. T. "Giftedness and the Education of the Gifted," in TRAVERS, R. M. W. (ed.). *Second Handbook of Research in Teaching.* Chicago: Rand McNally Co., 1973.

GOERTZEL, VICTOR, and GOERTZEL, MILDRED G. *Cradles of Eminence.* Boston: Little Brown & Co., 1962.

GOLDBERG, MIRIAM L. *Research on the Talented.* New York: Teachers College Press, 1965.

GOWAN, JOHN C. "Factors of Achievement in Schools and Colleges," *Journal of Counselling Psychology*, VII (1960), 91–95.

GOWAN, JOHN C., and DEMOS, GEORGE D. *The Education and Guidance of the Ablest.* Springfield, Ill.: Charles C. Thomas, 1964.

GRACE, HARVEY, and BOOTH, NANCY L. "Is the Gifted Child a Socially Isolate?" *Peabody Journal of Education*, XXXV (1958), 195–96.

GRAZIN, K. L., and GRAZIN, W. J. "Peer Group Choice as a Device for Screening Intellectually Gifted Children," *Gifted Child Quarterly*, XIII (1969), 183–94.

GROTH, NORMA J. "Differences in Parental Environment Needed for Degree Achievement for Gifted Men and Women," *Gifted Child Quarterly*, XV (1971), 256–59.

GUILFORD, J. P. "Three Faces of Intellect," *American Psychologist*, XIV (1969), 466–78.

HARGREAVES, HENRY L. "The Faculty of Imagination. An Inquiry Concerning the Existence of a General Faculty or Group Factor of Imagination," *British Journal of Psychology, Monograph Supplement No. 3*, 1927.

HAUCK, BARBARA B., and FREEHILL, MAURICE R. *The Gifted: Case Studies.* Dubuque: William C. Brown, 1972.

HILDRETH, GERTRUDE M. *Introduction to the Gifted.* New York: McGraw-Hill, 1966.

HOLLINGSWORTH, LETA S. *Children Above 180 I.Q.* New York: World Book Co., 1942.

HORNER, MARTINA. "The Motives to Avoid Success and Changing Aspirations of College Women," *Women on Campus*, 1970, pp. 12–23.

HUDSON, LIAM. *Contrary Imaginations*. London: Pelican Books, 1968.

HUGHES, H. HERBERT, and CONVERSE, HAROLD D. "Characteristics of the Gifted: A Case for a Sequel to Terman's Study," *Exceptional Children*, IV (1962), 179–83.

IMPELIZZERI, IRENE H., BARR, D. L., and CONNEY, I. E. "An Investigation of the Scholastic Functioning of 4875 High Ability Secondary School Students in New York City," in KORNRICH, M. L., *Underachievement*. Springfield, Ill.: Charles C. Thomas, 1965.

JACOBS, J. C. "Teacher Attitudes Toward Gifted Children," *Gifted Child Quarterly*, XVI (1972), 23–26.

KOMAROVSKY, MIRRA. "Cultural Contradiction and Sex Roles," *American Journal of Sociology*, LII: 3 (November, 1946), 184–89.

KRETCHMER, ERNST. *The Psychology of Men of Genius*. New York: The Macmillan Company, 1951.

KRUGMAN, MORRIS, and IMPELIZZERI, IRENE H. "Identification and Guidance of Underachieving Gifted Students in New York City," *Exceptional Children*, XXVI (1960), 283–86.

LAYCOCK, FRANK, and CAYLOR, JOHN S. "Physique of Gifted Children and Their Less Gifted Siblings," *Child Development*, XXXV (1964), 63–74.

LAYCOCK, SAMUEL R. *Gifted Children*. Toronto: Copp, Clark, 1957.

LEHMAN, HARVEY C. *Age and Achievement*. Princeton: Princeton University Press, 1953.

LOMBROSO, CESARE. *The Men of Genius*. London: Prentis, 1891.

MACKINNON, DONALD W. "The Nature and Nurture of Creative Talent," *American Psychologist*, XVII (1962), 484–95.

McGILLIVRAY, R. H. "Differences in Home Background Between High Achieving and Low Achieving Gifted Children: A Study of 100 Grade Eight Pupils in the City of Toronto Public Schools," *Ontario Journal of Educational Research*, VI (1964), 99–106.

MEAD, MARGARET. "The Gifted Child in the American Culture of Today," *Journal of Teacher Education*, V (1954), 211–14.

MEEKER, MARY N. *The Structure of Intellect: Its Uses and Implications*. Columbus, O.: Charles E. Merrill, 1969.

MEYER, W. J., and THOMPSON, G. C. "Sex Differences in the Distribution of Teacher Approval and Disapproval Among Sixth Grade Children," *Journal of Educational Research* XLIV (1959), 385–96.

MILES, T. ROBERT. "On Defining Intelligence," *British Journal of Educational Psychology*, XXVII (1957), 153–65.

MONDERER, J. H. "An Evaluation of Nebraska Program of Early Entrance to Elementary School," *Dissertation Abstracts*, XIV (1954), 633.

NICHOLS, ROBERT C. "Parental Attitudes of Intelligent Adolescents and Creativity of Their Children," *Child Development*, XXXV (1964), 1041–49.

NISBET, BERNARD L. *The Insanity of Genius*. London: McPiers, 1891.

OSGOOD, C. E., et al. *The Measurement of Meaning*. Urbana: University of Illinois Press, 1957.

O'SHEA, HARRIET E. "Friendship and the Intellectually Gifted Child," *Exceptional Children*, XXVI (1960), 327–35.

PASSOW, A. HARVEY, and GOLDBERG, MIRIAM L. *The Talented Youth Project: A Progress Report*. New York: Teachers College Press, 1961.

PEGNATO, W. CARL, and BIRCH, JACK W. "Locating Gifted Children in Junior High Schools," *Exceptional Children*, XXV (1959), 300–304.

PINTNER, RUDOLPH. "Intelligence and Its Measurement," *Journal of Educational Psychology*, XII (1921), 149–52.

POHL, R. GEORGE. "Teacher Nomination of Intellectualy Gifted Children in the Primary Grades," *Dissertation Abstracts International*, XXXI (1970), 22–37.

PRESSEY, SIDNEY L. "Educational Acceleration: Occasional Procedure or Major Issue?" *Personnel and Guidance Journal*, XLI (1962), 12–17.

PRINGLE, KELMER, M. L. *Able Misfits*. London: Longman, 1970.

ROE, ANNE. "A Psychologist Examines 64 Eminent Scientists," *Scientific American*, CLXXXVII (1952), 21–25.

ROSENTHAL, ROBERT, and JACOBSON, LENORE F. "Teachers' Expectancies: Determinants of Pupils' I.Q. Gains," *Psychological Reports*, XIX (1966), 115–18.

ROTHMAN, ESTHER, and LEVINE, M. P. "From Little League to Ivy League," *Educational Forum*, XXVIII (1963), 29–34.

SATO, I. S. "The Culturally Different Gifted Child – the Dawning of His Day," *Exceptional Children*, XL (1974), 572–76.

SCARPELLINI, CARLO. "Riverlazionni sugli alumni intellectualmente dotati: il guidizio scolastico e psicologico," *Contributi dell' Iustitato di psicologia*, XXIX (1967), 552–75.

SEARS, PAULINE S. *The Effect of Classroom Conditions on the Strength of Achievement Motive and Work Output of Elementary School Children*. Stanford: Stanford University Press, 1963.

SHAW, MERVILLE C., and McCUEN, JOHN T. "The Onset of Academic Underachievement in Bright Children," *Journal of Educational Psychology*, LI (1960), 103–8.

SHAW, MERVILLE C. "Note on Parental Attitudes Toward Independence Training and the Academic Achievement of Their Children," *Journal of Educational Psychology*, LV (1964), 371–74.

SHIMAN, M. F. *Individualized Learning*. London: Macmillan & Co., 1970.

SMILANSKY, MOSHE, and NEVO, DAVID. *Secondary Boarding School for Gifted Students From Disadvantaged Strata*. Tel-Aviv: Tel-Aviv University School of Education, 1971.

SMITH, P. G., and PRINDLE, V. T. "The Culturally Disadvantaged Pupil on Cumulative Record," *Journal of Negro Education*, XXXVIII (1969), 78–81.

STEWARD, FRANCIS A. "Measuring Intelligence," in ANASTASI, ANNE. *Differential Psychology*. New York: The Macmillan Company, 1958.

SULLEROT, EVELYNE. *Women, Society and Change*. New York: McGraw-Hill, 1971

TERMAN, LEWIS M. "Intelligence and Its Measurement," *Journal of Educational Psychology*, XII (1921), 131–35.

———. Mental and Physical Traits of a Thousand Gifted Children. (*Genetic Studies of Genius*, ed LEWIS M. TERMAN, Vol. I). Stanford: Stanford University Press, 1925.

———. "The Discovery and Encouragement of Exceptional Talent," *American Psychologist*, IX (1954), 221–30.

TERMAN, LEWIS M., and ODEN, MELITA H. *The Gifted Child Grows Up*. (*Genetic Studies of Genius*, ed. LEWIS M. TERMAN, Vol. IV.) Stanford: Stanford University Press, 1947.

———. *The Gifted Group at Mid-Life*. (*Genetic Studies of Genius*, ed. LEWIS M. TERMAN, Vol. V.) Stanford: Stanford University Press, 1959.

THISTLEWHITE, D. L. "The Conservation of Intellectual Talent," *Science*, CXXVIII (1958), 822–26.

THORNDIKE, EDWARD L. "Intelligence and Its Measurement," *Journal of Educational Psychology*, XII (1921), 124–27.

TOFFLER, ALVIN. *Future Shock*. New York: Harper & Row, 1970.

TORRANCE, E. PAUL. "Broadening Concepts of Giftedness in the '70's," *Gifted Child Quarterly*, XV (1971), 42–46.

WARREN, J. R., and HEIST, P. A. "Personality Attributes of Gifted College Students," *Science*, CXXXII (1960), 330–37.

WEISMAN, NOEMI. "Early School Admission of Gifted Children." Unpublished Master's dissertation, Bar Ilan University, 1972.

WEISS, LUDWIG. "Underachievement – Empirical Studies," *Journal of Adolescence*, III (1972), 143–51.

WHITEHEAD, ALFRED NORTH. *Aims of Education*. New York: The Macmillan Company, 1929.

———. "Preface" to DONHAM, W. B., *Business Adrift*. New York: McGraw-Hill, 1931.

WILEY, RUTH. *The Self Concept*. Lincoln: University of Nebraska Press, 1974.

WITTY, PAUL A. "A Genetic Study of Fifty Gifted Children," in *Iintelligence: its Nature and Nurture*. ("Thirty-Ninth Yearbook of the National Society for the Study of Education.") Bloomington, Ill.: Ohio State University Press, 1940.

WORCESTER, DEAN A. *The Education of Children of Above Average Mentality*. Lincoln: University of Nebraska Press, 1956.

YAMAMOTO, KAURO. "Effects of Restriction of Range and Test Unreliability on Correlation Between Measures of Intelligence and Creative Thinking," *British Journal of Educational Psychology*, XXXV (1965), 300–305.

ZIV, AVNER. "Children's Behaviour Problems as Viewed by Teachers, Psychologists and Children." *Child Development*, XLI (1970), 871–79.

———. *Psychological Aspects of Education* (Hebrew). Tel-Aviv: Yahdav, 1975.

———. "The Self Image of Underachieving Gifted Children." *Studies in Education*, III (1975), 141–48.

About the Author

Dr. Ziv obtained his PH.D. in Clinical Psychology at the Sorbonne. He has lectured and taught in North America, Europe and Asia, and has published writings in English, French and Hebrew on the subject of intellectually gifted children. He is now Director of the Counselling Program at Tel-Aviv University, Israel.